T0365944

ZALES

THE NEXT-GEN SALES PLAYBOOK

JANBI VAROKA

ARCHWAY
PUBLISHING

Archway Publishing books may be ordered through booksellers or by contacting:

Archway Publishing
1663 Liberty Drive
Bloomington, IN 47403
www.archwaypublishing.com
844-669-3957

Because of the dynamic nature of the Internet, any web addresses or links contained in
this book may have changed since publication and may no longer be valid. The views
expressed in this work are solely those of the author and do not necessarily reflect the
views of the publisher, and the publisher hereby disclaims any responsibility for them.

Any people depicted in stock imagery provided by Getty Images are
models, and such images are being used for illustrative purposes only.
Certain stock imagery © Getty Images.

ISBN: 978-1-6657-7591-5 (sc)
ISBN: 978-1-6657-7592-2 (e)

Library of Congress Control Number: 2025906717

Print information available on the last page.

Archway Publishing rev. date: 04/03/2025

CONTENTS

Foreword.. vii

Introduction: A Journey of Gratitude, Principles, and
    Transformation ix

Chapter 1: The Sales Mindset... 1
    Turning Challenges into Opportunities 5
    The Power of Adaptability.. 10
    The Art of Selling Partnership... 12
    Turning Challenges into Innovation 14
    The Tale of Two Shoes in the Digital Era................................ 17
Chapter 2: Masters of the Customer's Experience....................... 23
    The 4 Key Trends reshaping sales.. 35
Chapter 3: The 4-Legged Stool of Value Proposition: A
    Modern Framework for Sales Excellence 47
    Mute Button and Allies.. 57
Chapter 4: From the Right Bus to the Whole Journey: The
    Evolution of Sales Thinking... 59
    Sales Techniques That Actually Work for Gen Z..................... 66
    The ZHUZH Sales Technique 67
    From the Funnel to the Flywheel—A New Sales Model 73
    The Power of Marketing Theories in Sales............................... 74
Chapter 5: Introducing the S.A.L.E.S. Theory: Selling to the
    Limitless Generation 76
Chapter 6: The Right Roles, Not Roulette: How AI Fixes Sales
    Teams 121

Chapter 7: Beyond the Horizon... 146

Chapter 8: The Art of Happy Sales: Building Relationships in
a Modern World 165

Chapter 9: The New B2B Playbook: Selling in the Digital-First Era...176

Chapter 10: The Pirates of Sales: Charting a New Course in
the Digital World.. 204

Chapter 11: S.C.A.L.E. The Hack you Need to Close Faster 219

The Growth Tree Mindset: Balancing Roots & Fruits in the
Digital Age 231

Afterword: The Power of Sales... 237

FOREWORD

This book is born from a journey of hard work, growth, and the invaluable support of those who have walked alongside me. My story would not be complete without honoring the two pillars of strength who have shaped my path: my Parents and my wife. My Parent's unwavering belief in my potential and their wise guidance instilled in me a sense of discipline and purpose. My wife's steadfast support and boundless encouragement have been the foundation upon which I've built my career, giving me the strength to face challenges with resilience and determination.

I must also pay tribute to Pierre Chammas, a mentor who has been a compass throughout my professional life. His wisdom, clarity, and deep understanding of the art of sales provided me with tools and perspectives that have defined my career. Pierre taught me that every great achievement in sales stems not just from strategies or targets but from the relationships and trust we cultivate along the way.

INTRODUCTION

A Journey of Gratitude, Principles, and Transformation

This book is a treasure trove of **meaningful sales stories** designed specifically for Generation Z. It's not just about learning strategies, it's about igniting the drive to innovate, adapt, and thrive in the ever-changing world of sales.

Drawing on my 26 years' experience across more than 40 markets spanning different continents and cultures, I've sought to share captivating sales stories that hold valuable lessons. These lessons serve as a beacon for every generation, inspiring them to continually find new ways to sell while staying true to their values and maintaining quality.

During my tenure at McCain, one value resonated deeply with me and became a cornerstone of my philosophy: **"Good Ethics is Good Business."** This principle reminded me that true success in sales transcends numbers; it is rooted in integrity, fairness, and mutual respect. Ethics, I realized, is not just a moral compass—it is a business strategy that builds trust, fosters loyalty, and ensures sustainability in an ever-changing world. Strong values drive strong ventures, forming the foundation for enduring success.

Today, as the digital revolution transforms every facet of our lives, we find ourselves in a sales landscape that is both exciting and daunting.

Gone are the days of physical shelves; now, customers navigate **endless digital shelves** on platforms that offer infinite options. This shift has redefined the journey of sales. Where once the destination was the sole focus, today the journey matters just as much—if not more.

In this era of sprawling digital relationships, the role of sales teams has become more challenging than ever. Building trust in a world dominated by virtual interactions requires empathy, adaptability, and a renewed focus on the customer's journey. Sales professionals are no longer merely closing deals—they are crafting experiences, creating connections, and shaping loyalty in ways that transcend the transactional.

My career across the Middle East, Africa, and Asia has taught me that every market is unique, influenced by its cultural nuances, legal frameworks, and economic dynamics. These differences demand tailored strategies, a deep understanding of customer behaviors, and the ability to adapt with agility. As sales professionals, our goal is not to sell what we produce but to meet the customer's needs—aligning our offerings with their aspirations and pain points.

This book explores how sales must evolve to thrive in a complex, interconnected world. From building trust to delivering unforgettable experiences, I delve into the strategies and lessons that have shaped my approach to sales. I share insights gleaned from diverse markets, discuss the challenges of digital transformation, and highlight the importance of adaptability and emotional intelligence in navigating today's sales landscape.

Let us embark on this journey together, exploring how the timeless principles of ethics, trust, and empathy can drive success in an ever-evolving, technology-driven world. After all, in sales—as in life—it's not just about the destination but about the relationships and experiences we create along the way.

In creating this book, I had the privilege of leveraging cutting-edge tools like ChatGPT, which played a significant role in translating complex ideas into accessible language and providing fresh perspectives on modern sales strategies. Its ability to synthesize information and offer new insights has been invaluable in shaping the structure and content of this playbook.

ZALES isn't just a framework; it's a mindset—a way to connect, inspire, and deliver value in a world where the rules of engagement are constantly changing. I hope this book equips you with the tools and motivation to redefine what's possible in your sales journey. Together, let's embrace the limitless potential of innovation, creativity, and human connection.

Janbi Varoka

CHAPTER 1

The Sales Mindset

In a world where numbers tell a deeper story than words, Generation Z is building its own bridges into the world of sales. They don't just rely on gut feelings; they leverage the power of data to understand customer motivations and aspirations. Like digital psychologists, they delve into the depths of consumer behavior to deliver hyper-personalized experiences.

In contrast, the previous generation relied on intuition and emotion to build their business relationships. But in our fast-paced world, where information spreads like wildfire, content is king. Generation Z, the digital creators, craft captivating content that grabs attention and nourishes minds. They don't just sell products; they weave narratives that touch hearts and build trust.

But does this mean we forget the lessons of the past? Absolutely not. They learn from the wisdom of the previous generation, mastering the art of building genuine relationships founded in trust and mutual understanding. They blend the power of data with the magic of technology to create unforgettable marketing experiences – experiences that seamlessly integrate human warmth with artificial intelligence.

Imagine this: a squad of Gen Z friends casually scrolling TikTok, swapping unfiltered product reviews, sliding into brand DMs on

Instagram, and making snap buying decisions before you can even say, "checkout complete." Welcome to the world of Gen Z — the digital trailblazers who are rewriting the rules of sales and connection.

Born between 1997 and 2012, this generation isn't just a market segment; they're the trendsetters-in-chief, shaping culture, influencing households, and wielding a jaw-dropping $360 billion in spending power in the U.S. alone. And that's just scratching the surface — their influence transcends borders, reshaping global consumer landscapes faster than any generation before them. Gen Z isn't just the "younger crowd" anymore. They're digital natives who grew up with a smartphone in one hand and a world of information at their fingertips. From binge-watching YouTube tutorials to creating viral TikTok challenges, they've mastered the art of influencing and being influenced. But they're not just scrolling mindlessly — they're researching, comparing, and making savvy decisions. **In short, Gen Z doesn't just buy things; they shape the trends.**

Education is one of the cornerstones of success in the world of sales, acting as a transformative tool that bridges knowledge and results. In sales, education goes far beyond formal degrees or certificates; it's about continuously learning market trends, understanding customer needs, honing communication skills, and mastering product knowledge. When sales teams and individuals commit to learning, they gain insights that can drastically improve customer relationships, foster trust, and ultimately lead to long-term loyalty.

Educating customers is equally powerful. When a customer understands the benefits, functionality, and unique selling points of a product, they're not just making a purchase; they're making an informed decision. Take the example of frozen potatoes in Saudi Arabia—the shift from fresh potatoes to frozen was possible because McCain invested in educating the market about the benefits of frozen fries. By showcasing how frozen options could deliver consistent quality and operational efficiency, they transformed the perception of the product, creating a demand that grew exponentially over the years.

Moreover, education in sales builds confidence. A well-informed sales professional can engage in meaningful conversations, addressing customer concerns with ease and delivering solutions that feel customized and thoughtful. This approach leads to higher customer satisfaction and opens doors to more referrals, as satisfied customers often recommend products to their networks.

In the digital age, where information is easily accessible, customers expect transparency and reliability. Sales professionals who prioritize education, not only for themselves but for their clients, stand out as knowledgeable advisors rather than just sellers. This approach creates trust, credibility, and a lasting impact, proving that education isn't just a nice-to-have in sales, it's an essential investment that drives positive results across the board.

In my years working in sales, one story stands out as a perfect example of how a simple, practical solution can unlock unexpected growth. This particular moment happened while I was working in the Egyptian market, where we had six distinct flavors of cream-filled biscuits: Vanilla,

Chocolate, Strawberry, Banana, Orange, and Coconut. Each carton we shipped contained eight packs of a single flavor.

The challenge? The Egyptian market was filled with countless small kiosks, each with limited space and a cautious approach to stocking up. Expecting these kiosks to purchase six different cartons – one for each flavor – was simply unrealistic. Most kiosks couldn't afford to dedicate that much space, let alone commit to large orders of each flavor individually. We found ourselves with a great product but a significant barrier in reaching these smaller retailers.

That's when one of our sharp-eyed sales reps had an idea. While discussing strategies with our distributor, he proposed a solution that was both simple and game-changing: "Why not mix the flavors?" Instead of selling single-flavor cartons, we'd repackage them, combining two flavors in each carton. Suddenly, each carton was a mini-variety pack, giving kiosks a much more appealing offer – they could buy just one or two cartons and still offer their customers a choice of flavors.

With this new approach, kiosks began placing orders enthusiastically. No longer faced with an all-or-nothing choice, they could stock a few cartons with mixed flavors, attract a wider range of customers, and avoid the risk of unsold inventory.

The result was astounding. In just a short period, sales in the Egyptian market soared by 300%. This straightforward repackaging strategy opened doors to kiosks across the country, creating a win-win scenario for everyone involved. For us, it was a reminder that sometimes, the best sales strategy is simply seeing things from the customer's perspective and making it easier for them to say "yes."

Turning Challenges into Opportunities

Sometimes, the biggest wins come from the wildest mistakes. Here's a story about how one massive order mishap in Kuwait turned into a major market takeover.

Our distributor in Kuwait had ordered one container of frozen cakes in three flavors and two sizes – 600g and 300g – simple, right? But somewhere along the line, the purchasing manager totally misfired and placed an order for six containers of *each* flavor and size. So, when the shipment arrived, it was cake chaos. The distributor was in full panic mode – how on earth would they move all that?

But the Canadian supplier? He saw potential instead of a problem. He told the distributor, "This doesn't have to be a disaster. It's our chance to make a splash." With that perspective shift, they came up with a game-changing plan. They launched a two-month campaign filled with non-stop sampling events at every major retailer in Kuwait, paired with irresistible promos to get customers hooked. Their mission? Make the cakes unforgettable and impossible to resist.

And guess what? It was a massive hit. Within just four months, the distributor sold every last container. But it didn't stop there – demand skyrocketed. What started as a one-container-every-two-months product quickly became a three-container-a-month necessity. Thanks to a simple reframing of a "disaster" as a "chance," they ended up boosting brand loyalty and growing their share of the market.

So, the lesson? Sometimes, a so-called disaster is just a chance in disguise – it's all about how you spin it.

Selling Through the Unthinkable: Turning Grief into Opportunity: A Spark in the Funeral Tent

South Africa at the turn of the 21st century was grappling with a devastating AIDS epidemic. The crisis was so severe that it drastically shortened life expectancy and reshaped daily life. Every Sunday, communities gather under funeral tents to mourn loved ones lost to the disease or workplace tragedies. These tents became a symbol of collective grief—and unexpectedly, an unlikely gateway to innovation in sales.

Enter McCain, the global frozen foods company. At the time, South African households predominantly used fresh vegetables for cooking. McCain, having recently acquired frozen vegetable and potato processing plants in the country, faced a significant challenge: how to convince a market deeply rooted in tradition to embrace frozen vegetables. The concept of convenience and consistent quality felt foreign to many.

The breakthrough came from an unusual observation. Funeral tents, often filled with mourning families and neighbors, also hosted women peeling, chopping, and preparing fresh vegetables for large meals served to attendees. It was a time-consuming task, especially for a community already burdened by emotional and physical exhaustion.

McCain's sales team saw an opportunity where others might have seen none. They approached these gatherings not as moments of tragedy but as windows to introduce a solution. With frozen vegetables, the women could save time and effort, achieve consistent quality, and still prepare delicious meals for hundreds.

From Tears to Trends: Changing Minds One Meal at a Time

The idea took root. McCain began sponsoring funeral tents, providing not just frozen vegetables but also physical tents branded with their logo and messaging. These sponsorships offered a dual purpose: a practical benefit to grieving families and a platform for McCain to showcase its products in action. Week after week, more South Africans experienced the convenience and quality of McCain's frozen vegetables firsthand.

The trend caught on. What began in funeral tents spread to households across the country. Families started recognizing that frozen vegetables weren't just convenient; they were affordable, reliable, and a game-changer for busy lives. Supermarket shelves became the next frontier, with South Africans eagerly purchasing McCain products for their own kitchens.

The Lesson: Innovation in Sales is About Seeing the Unseen

This story isn't just about frozen vegetables. It's a masterclass in thinking outside the box—quite literally. McCain's ability to identify a sales channel in the most unexpected of places highlights the power of empathy, creativity, and adapting to the consumer's world. Even in the somber environment of a funeral tent, they found a way to provide value, connect with the community, and build lasting trust.

The takeaway is clear: Don't let traditional thinking confine your approach. Whether you're selling an idea, a product, or a vision, sometimes the most unconventional paths lead to the most impactful results.

From Tank to Table

Smart salesperson thrives in any situation, no matter how challenging or unconventional. They're always on the lookout for creative ways to sell and connect with their audience. One of the most striking examples of this comes from recent events in Syria—a story that's equal parts tragic and inspiring.

In the aftermath of the Syrian regime's fall, abandoned military equipment, including tanks, was left scattered across the streets. One particularly resourceful vendor saw an opportunity to turn a symbol of war into something entirely unexpected. He transformed a decommissioned tank into a vegetable stand. Yes, a **tank-turned-market-stall**, bridging the gap between the battlefield and the dining table.

This innovative move didn't just meet his business needs; it became a viral sensation on social media, capturing the world's attention. The tank, once an icon of conflict, was now a platform for peace, symbolizing resilience and the power of reinvention. By freezing the tank in time and using it as a humble food cart, the vendor told a story far greater than his products—it was a story of hope and creativity.

The lesson? A smart salesperson doesn't just sell; they create moments that spark curiosity, start conversations, and leave a lasting impression. They understand that every sale can tell a story, and every story can make an impact.

The Power of Adaptability

From Jeddah to Japan: How a Small Suggestion Saved McDonald's

It was the 1990s, and McDonald's had its sights set on entering the Middle Eastern market. To discuss supply chain logistics, a group of senior executives gathered in Jeddah, Saudi Arabia, for a pivotal meeting with Pierre Chammas, a representative of McCain Foods—and, coincidentally, my mentor.

The conversation seemed straightforward at first. The McDonald's team was focused on ensuring their iconic French fries could be supplied to the Middle Eastern market without disruption. But then, Pierre raised a point that left the room baffled: he suggested McDonald's alter one key ingredient in their fries—the beef tallow.

What is Beef Tallow, and Why Change It?

Beef tallow, a rendered fat from cows, was a hallmark of McDonald's fries. It gave them their signature rich flavor, crispy texture, and golden perfection. However, Pierre pointed out a critical issue: Saudi Arabia's halal regulations. Beef tallow could pose compliance risks and cultural concerns, particularly in the region's highly regulated and religiously observant market.

The McDonald's executives were skeptical. Why change a winning formula for just one region? They returned to the U.S., amused by the suggestion but intrigued enough to investigate. Eventually, after weighing the risks and benefits, McDonald's decided to create a Middle Eastern-specific recipe using plant-based oil instead of beef tallow.

Fast-Forward to the Unexpected Twist

Years later, the world faced a food crisis—the outbreak of mad cow disease in North America. These epidemic halted exports of beef-based products, including McDonald's fries, to key international markets like Japan. The situation was dire for McDonald's Japan, one of the company's largest franchises globally, as its fry supply was entirely dependent on U.S. and Canadian sources.

Amid the chaos, someone remembered the unique Middle Eastern recipe: plant-based fries with no beef tallow. This halal-compliant version had never relied on beef products and was unaffected by the crisis. Overnight, McDonald's began exporting the Middle Eastern fries to Japan, saving the franchise from a catastrophic supply chain failure.

A Lesson in Adaptability and Foresight

This small adjustment, born out of cultural sensitivity and regulatory awareness, turned out to be a lifesaver not just for McDonald's in Japan, but for its global operations. Over time, McDonald's adopted the plant-based recipe worldwide, replacing beef tallow with vegetable oil for all its fries.

The Moral of the Story

Think Globally, Act Locally: Understanding regional markets and adapting to their needs can have far-reaching benefits beyond initial expectations.

Small Changes Can Have Big Impacts: What seemed like a minor suggestion in Jeddah became a global solution during a crisis.

Foresight Wins the Day: Flexibility and openness to innovation, even when it challenges established norms, can future proof a business.

For Gen Z sales and business leaders, this story highlights the power of cultural awareness, proactive problem-solving, and a willingness to pivot. Sometimes, a seemingly small detail can reshape the trajectory of an entire global operation—and save the day when the unexpected strikes.

The Art of Selling Partnership

From Wings to Trust: How Emirates and Boeing Built a Partnership That Redefined Aviation

In the late 1990s, Emirates Airlines was a regional carrier with big dreams. Based in Dubai, a city that was itself on the brink of becoming a global hub, Emirates had a vision: to transform from a modest airline into a dominant global player. But to achieve this, the airline needed more than ambition—it needed the right aircraft, ones that could offer cutting-edge technology, fuel efficiency, and the flexibility to serve an increasingly diverse range of routes.

Two aviation giants, Boeing and Airbus, were vying for Emirates' attention. Both had stellar products, competitive pricing, and attractive financing options. On the surface, there wasn't much to distinguish them. But beneath the surface, Boeing was playing a very different game—one that wasn't just about planes but about partnerships.

Boeing didn't approach Emirates as just another customer. They understood that this was a company on a transformative journey, and they aimed to be a part of that vision. Phil Condit, Boeing's CEO at the time, led a team that focused not on selling planes but on understanding Emirates' long-term goals. It wasn't about specifications or contracts; it was about creating a shared future.

Executives from Boeing didn't limit their engagement to boardroom discussions. They flew to Dubai, spending time with Sheikh Ahmed bin Saeed Al Maktoum, Emirates' Chairman and CEO, and his team. These weren't rushed, transactional meetings. Instead, Boeing's representatives immersed themselves in Emirates' world, learning about the airline's operational challenges, its aspirations, and the unique dynamics of its market.

In return, Emirates' leadership was invited to Boeing's headquarters in Seattle. But this wasn't just a tour of the factory floor; it was a behind-the-scenes journey into the heart of aircraft innovation. The Emirates team witnessed how planes were designed, built, and tested, forging a deeper understanding of Boeing's capabilities—and, more importantly, a trust in their commitment.

The turning point came in 2001 at the Dubai Airshow, where Emirates placed a groundbreaking order for 58 Boeing aircraft valued at $15 billion. This wasn't just a business deal; it was a declaration of trust. Boeing had aligned itself so closely with Emirates' vision that the two companies were no longer just seller and buyers, they were partners.

But the story didn't end there. When Emirates needed an ultra-long-haul aircraft to connect Dubai with distant cities across the globe, Boeing didn't simply offer an existing model. Instead, they collaborated with Emirates to develop the 777-300ER, a plane tailored to the airline's specific needs. This wasn't just a sale; it was co-creation. The result was a game-changer for both companies, with Emirates becoming the largest operator of this wildly successful aircraft.

Today, the partnership between Boeing and Emirates stands as one of the most iconic in the aviation industry. It's a testament to the power of relationships in sales—not just superficial connections but genuine partnerships built on mutual respect and shared goals. Boeing didn't just deliver planes; they delivered trust, adaptability, and a willingness to invest in their partner's success.

The difference between being a good salesman and a great one. A good salesman hits targets and closes deals. A great salesman doesn't pitch products; he pitches partnerships. He doesn't just meet immediate needs; he anticipates future opportunities and aligns himself with his client's broader vision.

As Sheikh Ahmed bin Saeed Al Maktoum once said: "In aviation, success is not about flying planes; it's about building relationships that let you soar above challenges."

For the new generation of sales professionals, this story offers a timeless lesson: in an era of data, metrics, and automation, the human connection remains irreplaceable. People don't just buy products or services; they buy trust, commitment, and the promise of shared success. In sales, as in life, relationships are the wings that lift us higher.

Turning Challenges into Innovation

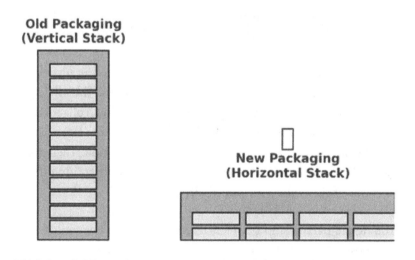

Old Packaging
(Vertical Stack)

New Packaging
(Horizontal Stack)

Old Price: 14 Pounds   New Price: 10 Pounds

Let me take you back to the early days of my career. I was working in the export department of a major confectionery and biscuit company in Saudi Arabia, riding the wave of opportunity created by the Free Arab Trade Agreement. One of our most exciting prospects was the Syrian market — a land full of potential, especially with zero customs duties on imported goods from Arab countries.

But like all good stories, there was a twist plot. The challenge wasn't entering the market; it was cracking the pricing code.

Here's the deal: a 140-gram biscuit pack that sold for 1 Riyal in Saudi Arabia couldn't be priced above 10 Syrian Pounds in Syria. At the time, 1 Riyal equaled 14 Syrian Pounds. And it wasn't just about exchange rates — the Syrian market was governed by a pricing rhythm. Everything needed to land on rounded numbers: 5, 10, or 15. Odd prices like 7 or 3? Forget it. They just didn't vibe with local buying habits.

For some, this would've felt like hitting a brick wall. But in sales, we don't see problems — we see challenges. Challenges don't stop you; they make you think, innovate, and grow.

Our export team brought this puzzle to production management, where the real tug-of-war began. The biscuits were packed in a vertical stack — 14 biscuits standing tall in a 140-gram pack. Production wasn't keen on changing the molds to create a smaller pack. Why? Because new molds meant big money and disrupted efficiency, driving up costs. It felt like a dead end.

But here's where the magic happened. In a moment I call "the spark of inspired clarity," an idea lit up the room.

What if we didn't change the biscuit itself but reimagined its presentation?

I proposed this: instead of stacking biscuits vertically, we could lay them horizontally, two biscuits side by side, stacked in pairs. This simple shift allowed us to create an 80-gram pack with eight biscuits. Not only was it the perfect size for Syrian pricing (10 Pounds), but it also gave us extra space for eye-catching branding. And then, we took it a step further by introducing a 40-gram pack with four biscuits, priced perfectly at 5 Pounds.

Here's where the magic doubled. We kept all six cream flavors from the original line and applied them to the new packs, creating a versatile and exciting product lineup.

To do this work, we needed a clear joint business plan — a single-page, no-fluff roadmap that laid out the strategy. We partnered with a strong local distributor, rolled out the new products, and let the market do the talking.

The results? Within two years, the Syrian market accounted for 10% of our factory's total production.

This wasn't just a win; it was a masterclass in innovation. We didn't overhaul everything — we reimagined what already existed.

For Gen Z, this is the takeaway: in sales, the answers don't always lie in tearing down and starting over. Sometimes, it's about seeing the same puzzle through a new lens. It's about adapting to the beat of your audience while staying true to your business goals.

Innovation isn't reserved for grand gestures. It's in the small, clever tweaks that turn challenges into opportunities. In the end, that's what makes you stand out — and that's where success lives.

The Tale of Two Shoes in the Digital Era

One of the most powerful sales techniques that has evolved with this new landscape is The Two Shoes Sales Technique. Originally a simple method used in physical retail, this approach has been transformed into a psychological principle that now shapes the way brands, AI-driven platforms, and social commerce engage with customers.

From Physical Sales to Digital Sales Psychology

Decades ago, the Two Shoes Technique was a go-to strategy for salespeople in physical stores. The premise was simple: instead of overwhelming the customer with too many options, the salesperson would present just two choices and ask:

"Which one do you prefer?"

If the customer hesitated and asked for a third option, the salesperson wouldn't just grab another product. Instead, they would ask:

"Which one didn't you like, and why?"

By doing this, the salesperson gathered valuable customer insights, fine-tuned the offering, and positioned the third option as the perfect solution—making it easier for the customer to say yes.

Fast forward to today, and this technique has gone far beyond the sales floor. In an era where customers are bombarded with choices online, the challenge is no longer lack of options—it's decision paralysis. This is where the Two Shoes Technique has evolved into a digital sales principle that reshapes the way businesses sell without selling.

How the Two Shoes Technique Applies to the Digital Age

a.   AI-Driven Recommendations: The Digital Salesperson

❖   From Salesperson to Algorithm:
      In the past, a good salesperson would narrow down choices for the customer. Today, AI does the same thing—but faster and more accurately.

Example: Netflix & Spotify

Instead of showing users thousands of movies or songs, Netflix and Spotify use personalized AI-driven recommendations to narrow down choices to just two or three best-fit options—just like a traditional salesperson would do in a store.

Example: Amazon & Zalando

Instead of forcing users to scroll through endless pages of products, Amazon and Zalando curate "Best Picks for You" based on browsing history, past purchases, and user behavior.

Sales Strategy:

- Use AI-powered recommendation engines to limit options for customers.
- Present two or three curated choices instead of overwhelming them.
- Make the decision feel effortless and intuitive.

b. Guided Sales Funnels: Replicating the In-Store Experience

- From Face-to-Face Interaction to Digital Journey:
A great salesperson in a store asks the right questions to guide a customer to the perfect product. Today, digital sales funnels do the same thing—without the customer ever interacting with a human.

Example: Apple's Website

Instead of overloading customers with every product variation, Apple's website guides users through a step-by-step selection process:

"Do you need a laptop for work or creativity?"
"Do you prefer lightweight or high-performance?"

Each answer narrows the choices until the customer lands on the perfect product—mirroring the Two Shoes Technique digitally.

Sales Strategy:

- Use interactive quizzes to guide customers toward the right product.
- Provide side-by-side comparisons of two or three options.
- Build progressive forms that filter options based on preferences.

---

c. Subscription-Based Models: Simplifying the Buying Decision

❖ From One-Time Sales to Continuous Engagement:

Subscription models have redefined how companies approach sales. Instead of customers making a single big decision, they now opt into smaller, ongoing commitments that feel less risky.

Example: SaaS Companies (Salesforce, HubSpot, Shopify)

Instead of offering ten different pricing tiers, top SaaS companies limit options to two or three key plans, making it easier for customers to decide.

Example: Meal Subscription Services (HelloFresh, Blue Apron)

Instead of letting customers get lost in a sea of meal options, these companies curate a selection based on preferences—ensuring customers never feel overwhelmed.

Sales Strategy:

- Offer fewer, well-defined pricing tiers instead of complex options.
- Make the first step low-risk (free trial, money-back guarantee).
- Focus on customer retention rather than just acquisition.

---

d.   Social Commerce & Influencer Marketing: Selling Without Selling

From Traditional Advertising to Social Proof:

Today's consumers don't trust traditional ads—they trust social proof, recommendations, and influencers. The best sales tactics don't feel like sales at all.

Example: Instagram & TikTok Influencers

Instead of overloading followers with a full catalog, top influencers use the Two Shoes Technique by presenting just two or three options and saying:

"Here are my top two favorite sneakers—help me decide which one I should get!"

"Which one would you pick?"

This engages followers, creates social proof, and removes the pressure of direct selling.

Sales Strategy:

- Use social proof and influencer marketing to showcase limited options.
- Engage customers through polls, Q&As, and comparison posts.
- Create scarcity & exclusivity to encourage faster decision-making.

The Future of Sales: Less is More

The biggest mistake companies make today isn't offering bad products, it's offering too many choices without direction. Customers don't need more options they need the right options.

Conclusion: The Sales Mindset – Turning Obstacles into Opportunities

Sales isn't just about transactions, it's about adaptability, resilience, and the ability to see opportunities where others see roadblocks. Whether it's repackaging biscuits for a challenging market, transforming an order mishap into a market takeover, or introducing a product in the most unexpected settings, the best salespeople don't wait for opportunities— they create them.

What sets successful sales professionals apart is their mindset. They don't fear problems; they embrace them as fuel for innovation. They think like strategists, act like storytellers, and build relationships that go beyond a single deal. In the end, sales aren't about pushing a product, it's about understanding, adapting, and delivering value in ways that are both creative and impactful.

As you move forward in your sales journey, ask yourself:

❖ Are you reacting to challenges, or are you shaping them into opportunities?
❖ Are you selling a product, or are you solving a problem?
❖ Are you waiting for the right conditions, or are you creating them?

The best sales stories—the ones that change industries and build legacies—come from those who see beyond the obstacles and into the possibilities.

CHAPTER 2

Masters of the Customer's Experience

Frappuccino your Business (Frenzy)

It's hard to imagine summer without the icy, creamy bliss of a Starbucks Frappuccino® with that iconic green straw. But rewind to 1993, and Starbucks was still just a handful of stores — no summer Frappuccino craze in sight. At that time, the company had fewer than 300 stores, mostly in northern cities. But Dina Campion, a Starbucks veteran managing the Southern California stores, had an idea that would change everything.

"It was a super hot summer, and we saw other local coffee spots blending cold coffee drinks," Campion remembers. "A few managers and I thought, why isn't Starbucks doing this?" Inspired by LA's love for cold drinks, she reached out to a former colleague, Dan Moore, now working at Starbucks HQ. He managed to get a blender shipped down, and they started testing the first Frappuccino at a single store in the San Fernando Valley.

The experiment was a hit, and soon the R&D team in Seattle was refining the recipe. By the summer of 1994, stores across Campion's district were serving up blended coffee drinks to enthusiastic customers. But there was still something missing: a memorable name. Just in time, Starbucks acquired a Boston coffee shop chain called The Coffee Connection – which had a slushy, soft-serve coffee drink they called "Frappuccino." The name stuck, and Starbucks prepped for a full U.S. launch.

Summer 1995 arrived, and Starbucks rolled out Frappuccino nationwide, with Coffee and Mocha flavors. The response? Insane. Starbucks tracked 200,000 drinks sold in the first week alone – double their expectations. Soon, the numbers were skyrocketing to 800,000 Frappuccinos per week, from Chicago to Boston. The Frappuccino wasn't just a summer hit; it filled stores during slower afternoons and attracted customers who weren't typical coffee drinkers. Sales soared, contributing to 11% of Starbucks' summer sales and pushing the company's stock to new highs.

But the Frappuccino story didn't end there. In 1996, Starbucks partnered with Pepsi to launch bottled Frappuccino drinks in stores, skipping the test phase entirely. And as demand continued to grow, Starbucks rolled out new flavors like Caramel Frappuccino, introduced dome lids and whipped cream, and even launched Frappuccino Blended Crème for non-coffee fans. Today, you can find Frappuccinos in more than 36,000 combinations worldwide, from Coffee Jelly Frappuccino in Asia to Brigadeiro Frappuccino in Brazil.

Howard Schultz captured it best: "Frappuccino epitomizes the spirit of Starbucks. It's experimental, adventurous, and engages people's imaginations." Now, it's more than just a drink – it's a piece of Starbucks history.

Let's brew up a fresh buzz language inspired by "Frappuccino" to energize your business culture and highlight creativity and innovation. By using terms that capture the unique, playful essence of the Frappuccino, you can create a vibrant vocabulary that connects with your team and customers alike. Here's how you can do it:

1. Frappuccino Effect

   - Meaning: The unexpected, but powerful, boost a product or idea gives to your brand, like how the Frappuccino transformed Starbucks.
   - Usage: "We're hoping our new product will have the Frappuccino Effect, driving engagement and filling a gap in the market."

2. Frappuccino Factor

   - Meaning: The blend of creativity, customer appeal, and market timing that makes a product irresistible.
   - Usage: "When designing new products, we're always looking for the Frappuccino Factor to make them stand out."

3. Frappuccino Moment

   - Meaning: The pivotal moment when an idea or product concept takes off unexpectedly.
   - Usage: "The team had a Frappuccino Moment when we realized how much customers loved the new limited edition."

4. Frappuccino Mindset

   - Meaning: An innovative approach that involves taking risks and reimagining traditional concepts.
   - Usage: "To stay ahead, we need to adopt a Frappuccino Mindset, continuously thinking about what could surprise and delight our customers."

5.   Frappuccino Fusion

- Meaning: The blend of various elements (like flavors, technologies, or departments) to create something unique and engaging.
- Usage: "This project is a Frappuccino Fusion of our marketing, tech, and product teams to deliver something groundbreaking."

6.   Frappuccino Wave

- Meaning: The wave of popularity and excitement that comes with launching a hit product.
- Usage: "We're riding the Frappuccino Wave with our new product launch this summer."

7.   Frappuccino Formula

- Meaning: A unique approach or "secret recipe" that captures consumer attention, much like the Frappuccino's blend of flavors and appeal.
- Usage: "The Frappuccino Formula is all about crafting products that people didn't know they wanted until they tried them."

8.   Frappuccino Frenzy

- Meaning: The intense demand or excitement around a product, driven by creativity, limited editions, or seasonal offerings.
- Usage: "Our new collection sparked a Frappuccino Frenzy; we sold out within hours of launch!"

9.   Frappuccino Legacy

- Meaning: A product or idea that continues to drive growth and brand identity over time.

- Usage: "This initiative could become our Frappuccino Legacy, something that represents our brand's values for years."

10. Frappuccino Effect

- Meaning: The impact of offering a product that diversifies your customer base and fills untapped demand.
- Usage: "We're aiming for a Frappuccino Effect by introducing something that will bring in new customers and enhance loyalty."

"A value proposition that wins today doesn't just solve problems, it creates unforgettable experiences, earns unshakable trust, and evolves alongside the buyer's journey."

Transforming Sales Through Customer Experience

The Seamless Solar Solution (Africa)

In rural Kenya, a solar energy company called Bright Sun Solutions recognized a pressing need: thousands of households lacked reliable electricity but couldn't afford expensive upfront costs for solar panels. Instead of using a one-size-fits-all sales strategy, Bright Sun focused on understanding their customers' unique challenges.

The company introduced a pay-as-you-go model. Sales agents, fluent in local languages and customs, visited villages, demonstrating how their solar panels worked. But the real innovation was the experience. They empowered customers by using mobile money systems like M-Pesa, allowing families to pay small, affordable installments.

One customer, Mary, shared how this tailored solution transformed her life. She could light her home, charge her phone, and keep her children safe after dark. The local sales agent didn't just sell her a product; they stayed in touch, offering troubleshooting tips via WhatsApp and ensuring her satisfaction.

Mary's glowing review spread through her village, driving word-of-mouth referrals. BrightSun didn't just sell solar panels, they created trust and loyalty by prioritizing Mary's experience. Their sales skyrocketed, and villages that were once hesitant to adopt solar now actively sought out BrightSun.

The Personalized Tea Journey (Asia)

In China, an emerging premium tea brand, Green Harmony, wanted to stand out in a crowded market. Instead of pushing products with discounts, they focused on crafting personalized tea experiences.

A customer, Liu Wei, visited a Green Harmony store in Shanghai. Instead of being overwhelmed with options, she was greeted by a "Tea Guide" who asked her about her taste preferences, lifestyle, and even her favorite time to drink tea. The guide curated a selection of teas and suggested pairing them with specific snacks. Liu Wei enjoyed a small, complimentary tea-tasting session that felt more like a spa experience than a sales pitch.

What set Green Harmony apart was the follow-up. After her visit, Liu Wei received a beautifully designed booklet about the teas she purchased, complete with brewing instructions. A week later, she got a message through WeChat from the Tea Guide, checking in on her experience and offering discounts on refill packages.

Liu Wei shared her story on social media, praising the thoughtful and personalized experience. Her post went viral, drawing hundreds of new customers to Green Harmony stores. By focusing on creating a connection and delighting the customer, Green Harmony didn't just sell tea—they built a loyal community.

The Lesson

In both Africa and Asia, these companies succeeded not by focusing on products alone but by creating exceptional customer experiences. By understanding local needs, personalizing the journey, and building trust, they turned one-time buyers into lifelong advocates. In today's world, customer experience isn't just part of the sales process, it is the sales process.

Here are two deeper and more meaningful customer experience stories from Africa and Asia that highlight the moral importance of customer-centric sales processes and their broader impact:

The Community Water Solution (Africa)

In Tanzania, a startup called LifeSpring Pumps sought to tackle a serious issue: access to clean drinking water. While many organizations had tried to sell water pumps to rural communities, they often failed because they didn't understand the daily struggles of the villagers. The pumps were either too expensive, too difficult to maintain, or simply didn't meet the community's needs.

LifeSpring took a different approach. Instead of just selling pumps, they spent months living among the villagers, listening to their stories. They learned that the biggest issue wasn't just clean water—it was the exhausting daily trek women and children had to make to distant water sources.

LifeSpring's sales strategy was not about products but empowerment. They designed an affordable, durable pump system and included a microfinancing plan so families could pay for small increments. But the true magic came in how they introduced the product. LifeSpring partnered with local leaders to host storytelling sessions where women shared how the pumps had freed up hours of their day. They could now spend that time earning money, farming, or ensuring their children go to school.

One of the first customers, Mama Amina, explained, "This pump gave us more than water; it gave us time, dignity, and hope." The company's sales grew rapidly—not because of aggressive tactics, but because they valued humanity over profit. LifeSpring's success showed how putting the customer's real-life struggles first can create not just sales but societal change.

The Farmer's Revival (Asia)

In rural India, a company called AgriLift set out to help struggling farmers increase their crop yields. For years, farmers had been sold fertilizers and pesticides by companies that promised high yields but failed to account for the region's unique soil and climate conditions. Many farmers went into debt, and some lost everything.

AgriLift's sales approach was radically different. They didn't push products; instead, they built trust through education. Their sales team began by offering free soil testing and workshops on sustainable farming practices. Farmers were taught how to rotate crops, conserve water, and use natural fertilizers. AgriLift also developed a mobile app in multiple regional languages, providing real-time weather updates and advice on planting schedules.

One farmer, Ramesh, was skeptical at first. He had been burned before by flashy sales pitches and empty promises. But after attending an AgriLift workshop, he decided to try their organic fertilizer. Within one season, Ramesh saw a 30% increase in his crop yield. The sales agent who worked with him didn't just disappear after the sale; they visited regularly, offering guidance and moral support.

Ramesh's success inspired his entire village to embrace AgriLift's methods. The company didn't just sell a product, they restored dignity and hope to an entire community. Their sales skyrocketed, but the real impact was seen in reduced farmer suicides and improved rural livelihoods. AgriLift became a symbol of how ethical and customer-focused sales can rebuild trust and transform lives.

The Moral Lesson

Both stories highlight a fundamental truth: sales isn't just about transactions; it's about transformation. Companies that take the time to truly understand their customers' struggles, respect their dignity, and prioritize their long-term well-being create not just profits but profound, lasting impact. In today's world, where many people have grown weary of hollow sales pitches, these examples from Africa and Asia remind us that authenticity and care are the ultimate competitive advantages.

Sales is, at its core, human practice rooted in understanding, connection, and trust between people. Despite advancements in technology and automation, the human element in sales remains irreplaceable. Here are modern insights into why and how embracing the humanity of sales makes it more effective in today's world:

1. **Sales are About Stories, Not Just Transactions**

Humans are wired for stories. In today's sales world, success isn't about listing features and benefits; it's about telling compelling stories that resonate emotionally. A salesperson who shares a story about how a product solved a similar problem for another customer creates a sense of relatability and trust.

For example, instead of saying, "Our product improves productivity by 20%," a salesperson might say, "One of our clients, a small business owner in Mumbai, was struggling to manage her growing customer base. With our solution, she not only grew her business but had more time for her family."

2. Empathy is the Core Skill

Sales is about understanding human emotions and motivations. Customers aren't just buyers; they're people with needs, fears, and aspirations. Empathy allows sales professionals to step into the customer's shoes, truly understand their pain points, and offer solutions that feel personal.

In a competitive market, empathy sets a salesperson apart. A customer who feels heard and understood is far more likely to buy, even if the product isn't the cheapest option. This is particularly true in markets like Asia and Africa, where relationships often outweigh price considerations.

3. Trust is the Currency of Sales

In a world flooded with options, trust has become the cornerstone of sales. People buy from people they trust, and building that trust requires transparency, integrity, and genuine care.

For instance, in rural Kenya, customers often rely on word-of-mouth recommendations rather than advertisements. A salesperson who goes the extra mile to ensure a customer understands the product—without pushing for an immediate sale—builds long-term credibility, leading to repeat business and referrals.

4. The Power of Human Connection in a Digital World

Technology has revolutionized sales, but it has also depersonalized many interactions. A live chat may answer questions, but it rarely builds relationships. The most effective salespeople combine the efficiency of digital tools with the warmth of human connection.

For example:

- A follow-up call after a virtual product demo.

- A handwritten thank-you note after a sale.
- Remembering personal details, like a client's birthday or their child's name, and mentioning them during interactions.

These small, human touches stand out in a sea of automated emails and generic follow-ups.

5. Collaboration, Not Selling

Modern sales is less about convincing someone to buy and more about working with them to solve a problem. It's a collaborative process where the salesperson acts as a partner, not a pusher.

Take the example of a technology company in Southeast Asia. Instead of presenting pre-packaged solutions, their sales team co-creates solutions with clients. They involve customers in brainstorming sessions, asking, "What challenges are you facing?" This co-creation approach not only results in better solutions but also makes the customer feel valued and respected.

6. Sales is a Relationship, Not a One-Time Deal

Today's successful salespeople know that customer lifetime value is more important than closing a single deal. Building strong, authentic relationships ensures customers keep coming back.

7. Cultural Sensitivity in Human Sales

Sales is deeply influenced by culture, especially in markets like Africa and Asia. Successful salespeople understand and respect these cultural nuances:

- In Asia, building relationships often precedes business deals. A salesperson who rushes the process may lose the deal entirely.

- In many African markets, community dynamics matter. A product may be judged not just on its merits but on how it benefits the broader community.

By respecting cultural norms and values, salespeople can deepen their human connections and build long-lasting trust.

How Human-Centric Sales is Effective Today

a. Stronger Customer Loyalty: Customers are more likely to stay loyal to brands that treat them as individuals rather than transactions.

b. Higher Referrals: Human connections lead to word-of-mouth marketing, which is especially powerful in closely-knit communities.

c. Resilience Against Competition: In markets flooded with options, human connection becomes a unique selling point.

d. Better Problem-Solving: Salespeople who engage deeply with customers can anticipate problems and offer tailored solutions.

e. Increased Brand Value: A company that prioritizes humanity in its sales process builds a reputation that goes beyond its products.

In a world driven by AI, automation, and data, the heart of sales remains unshakably human. It's about listening, connecting, and building trust. While technology can enhance efficiency, the true power of sales lies in understanding and responding to the human experience. After all, people don't just buy products, they buy solutions, emotions, and relationships.

The 4 Key Trends reshaping sales

The future is here—and it's more personal, purposeful, and powerful than ever. Let's go make it happen.

1. Artificial Intelligence (AI) and Automation: The Future of Sales Starts Here

AI and automation are no longer futuristic buzzwords; they're the tools transforming sales right now. While these technologies have been around for years, advancements in generative AI (like ChatGPT) are pushing them into the mainstream. They're making sales smarter, faster, and more personalized—and if you're not already using them, you're leaving opportunities on the table.

The Era of Intelligent Sales

A recent study by Pipedrive reveals that 33% of sales and marketing professionals use AI daily, and 83% have implemented some form of automation. These numbers are growing rapidly as AI becomes a must-have for any forward-thinking sales team. Why? Because sales reps using AI-powered tools are closing deals at a 9.8% higher rate than those without them.

AI isn't just a tool; it's your new partner in success. Let's explore how it's revolutionizing sales with real-world examples and actionable tips.

How to Get Started with AI in Sales

> **Start Small:**
> Don't try to implement everything at once. Pick one or two AI tools, like a lead-scoring platform or a chatbot, and see how they impact your workflow.

➢ **Train Your Team:**

AI is only as good as the people using it. Invest in training so your sales team understands how to leverage these tools effectively.

➢ **Measure and Adjust:**

Track how AI impacts your KPIs, such as conversion rates or time spent per lead. Use these insights to refine your approach.

➢ **Stay Curious:**

The AI landscape is evolving rapidly. Stay informed about new tools and trends and be ready to experiment.

AI and automation are reshaping sales, making it smarter, faster, and more human-centric. But remember: AI is a tool, not a replacement for the personal touch that makes sales truly successful. The key is finding balance-leveraging technology to enhance, not replace, your relationships with customers.

2. Beyond AI: The Power of Data-Driven Sales

While AI plays a crucial role in modern sales, it's only part of a bigger picture. Data analytics and insights are taking center stage, shaping how businesses understand customers, predict trends, and optimize sales strategies. In today's fast-paced market, raw data isn't enough—it's about transforming it into actionable insights that drive smarter decisions and better customer experiences.

- Predictive Analytics and Sales Forecasting: Selling Smarter

Predictive analytics is revolutionizing sales by using historical data, machine learning, and AI to forecast future outcomes. Think of it as a crystal ball for sales reps—except it's powered by numbers, not magic.

Real-World Example: Walmart's Big Data Revolution

Walmart collects over 2.5 petabytes of data every hour from more than 1 million customers. This data helps the retail giant optimize everything from product assortment to shelf placement, ensuring customers get what they need when they need it.

For example, Walmart used predictive analytics to anticipate a spike in strawberry Pop-Tart sales ahead of a hurricane. Why? Historical data showed people stocked up on comfort food before storms. Walmart preemptively stocked its shelves, resulting in record sales.

How Predictive Analytics Elevates Sales

A. Spotting Hidden Opportunities

AI tools analyze massive datasets to identify leads that sales reps might overlook.

- Example: A B2B software company used predictive analytics to analyze historical deal data. They discovered that clients who downloaded a specific whitepaper were 40% more likely to convert. Armed with this insight, the sales team focused on nurturing those leads, boosting their closing rates by 20%.

Practical Tip: Use tools like Salesforce Einstein or Zoho Analytics to uncover patterns in your data. These platforms can rank leads by their likelihood to convert, helping you prioritize your time and energy.

B. Accurate Sales Forecasting

Gone are the days of intuition-driven forecasts. Data analytics tools now create precise sales predictions based on historical trends and current market conditions.

- Example: PepsiCo implemented predictive analytics to forecast demand for its products. By analyzing seasonal trends and consumer behavior, the company optimized its supply chain, reduced waste, and ensured stores were always stocked with high-demand items.

Practical Tip: Integrate predictive tools into your CRM to forecast sales and identify high-value opportunities. Tools like Microsoft Power BI can provide clear, actionable insights into your pipeline.

Unlocking the Power of Sales Data

a. AI-Boosted BI Platforms

Business intelligence (BI) platforms are becoming smarter, thanks to AI. Imagine a dashboard that doesn't just display data but actively suggests your next best action.

- Example: Microsoft Power BI now uses machine learning to identify trends and offer recommendations. For instance, it might tell you, "Follow up with Client X—they've shown increased activity on your website."

Practical Tip: Train your team to use BI tools for real-time insights. Make it a habit to review these dashboards daily for immediate course corrections.

b. Predictive ERPs

Enterprise Resource Planning (ERP) systems aren't just for tracking inventory anymore. They're becoming predictive tools that can adjust your sales strategies in real time.

- Example: A clothing retailer used an AI-powered ERP to predict a drop in demand for winter jackets due to an unusually warm season. They shifted their focus to promoting lighter apparel and avoided overstock issues.

Practical Tip: Pair your ERP with predictive tools to align inventory and sales efforts. Ensure your sales and ops teams are working from the same data to stay agile.

c. Unified Data Ecosystems

Sales data is often siloed from marketing, finance, and operations. A unified ecosystem breaks down these walls, giving sales teams a complete view of the business.

- Example: A SaaS company synchronized its sales and marketing data, uncovering that customers who attended webinars were 30% more likely to renew their contracts. This insight led to targeted follow-ups and higher retention rates.

Practical Tip: Invest in platforms like HubSpot or Tableau that integrate data from multiple departments. The goal is to create a 360-degree view of your customers and their journey.

d. Conversational Data Queries

The days of navigating complex systems to extract insights are over. With conversational AI, you can simply ask, "What are my top-performing products in the Midwest this quarter?"

- Example: Tools like ThoughtSpot allow users to query data in plain language, making insights accessible to everyone, not just data analysts.

Practical Tip: Explore conversational analytics platforms and train your team to use them. They're especially helpful during sales meetings when quick answers are needed.

How to Capitalize on the Data Trend

a. Start with Clean Data:

Messy or incomplete data leads to bad decisions. Make sure your CRM is updated and accurate.

b. Invest in Training:

Data tools are only useful if your team knows how to use them. Provide ongoing training to ensure they're confident with analytics platforms.

c. Set KPIs:

Use data to track key performance indicators like close rates, customer acquisition costs, and churn. Let the numbers guide your strategy.

d. Stay Curious:

Keep experimenting. Data trends and tools are constantly evolving, and staying on top of them can give you a significant competitive edge.

Data isn't just numbers on a screen, it's your roadmap to better sales. By embracing predictive analytics, unified data systems, and conversational tools, you'll not only stay ahead of the competition but also provide a superior experience for your customers.

3. Social Selling: Turning Likes into Leads

Let's face it—if you're not selling on social media, you're already behind. Platforms like LinkedIn, Instagram, and even TikTok aren't just for scrolling memes or stalking your high school crush—they're where deals are happening, trends are forming, and trust is being built. Social selling isn't about shouting, "Buy my product!" into the void. It's about sliding into your prospects' feeds, building real connections, and becoming the go-to expert they can't stop following.

Why Social Selling Works

Here's the deal: 87% of sales reps say social selling works. And it makes sense. Everyone is online, from your favorite barista to the CEO of that company you've been awaiting. Social selling meets people where they are and engages them in a way that feels natural, not salesy.

It's about:

- Finding leads who don't even know they need you (yet).
- Showing off your expertise without coming across like a know-it-all.
- Keeping up with your buyers without being "that" pushy salesperson.
- Spotting trends and pain points in real time.

Story: How a TikTok Saved a Deal

Picture this: Sarah, a sales rep at a SaaS company, was struggling to close a deal with a tech startup. Her emails went unanswered, and her calls were ghosted. But then, she noticed the CEO posting quirky TikToks about productivity hacks. Sarah decided to jump in on the fun, creating a short, clever video explaining how her software could solve their bottleneck issues.

The result? The CEO slid into her DMs, complimented her creativity, and booked a meeting. Two weeks later, Sarah closed a $50,000 deal—all because she leaned into TikTok's casual vibe and met the client on their turf.

Lesson: Sales isn't always about formal pitches. Sometimes, it's about being where your audience is and speaking their language.

How to Crush It in Social Selling

a. Build Your Personal Brand

Your social media profiles are your storefronts. Whether it's LinkedIn for B2B connections or Instagram for lifestyle products, people need to know who you are and what you stand for.

- Example: Check out Gary Vaynerchuk (GaryVee). He doesn't just sell; he shares. His content is about marketing tips, motivation, and authenticity. That's why people trust him—and why his businesses thrive.

Practical Tip: Optimize your LinkedIn bio. Make it clear what you do, who you help, and why they should connect with you. Use a professional photo, but don't be afraid to let your personality shine in your posts.

b. Engage, Don't Spam

Nobody likes a cold DM that screams, "BUY MY PRODUCT." Instead, start conversations. Comment on posts, share insights, and genuinely interact with your audience.

- Example: A financial advisor started replying to tweets from small business owners asking for tips on cash flow. By offering free advice and sharing relevant articles, she became a trusted resource—and eventually landed five new clients.

Practical Tip: Spend 15 minutes a day engaging with your network. Leave thoughtful comments, ask questions, and share content that adds value.

c. **Be a Content Machine**

Posting once in a blue moon isn't going to cut it. To stand out, you need to consistently create content that informs, entertains, or inspires.

- Example: A cybersecurity consultant shared weekly LinkedIn posts about common online scams. One post about a phishing scam went viral, generating thousands of views and a handful of leads from companies worried about their own vulnerabilities.

Practical Tip: Use the 80/20 rule: 80% of your posts should provide value (like tips, insights, or stories), and 20% can promote your product or service.

d. **Choose the Right Platforms**

Not all platforms are created equal. LinkedIn is gold for B2B, while Instagram and TikTok shine for visual products or services targeting younger audiences.

- Stats You Need to Know:

  o LinkedIn: 70% of sales reps say it's the best platform for connecting with customers.
  o Facebook: Still relevant for 38% of sales pros.
  o Instagram: Perfect for the 31% targeting visually driven consumers.
  o YouTube: Great for sharing deep-dive content (29%).

Practical Tip: Pick 1-2 platforms where your audience hangs out and focus your efforts there. You don't have to be everywhere—just where it matters.

e. **Track Trends and Pain Points**

Social media is a goldmine for figuring out what's on your buyers' minds. Follow hashtags, read comments, and use tools like LinkedIn Sales Navigator to spot trends.

- Example: A sales rep at a logistics company noticed a surge in posts about shipping delays. She created a whitepaper on "How to Navigate Supply Chain Challenges in 2024" and shared it on LinkedIn. It brought in dozens of inquiries from businesses struggling with similar issues.

Practical Tip: Set up alerts for industry-specific hashtags or keywords. Use platforms like Hootsuite or Sprout Social to monitor conversations and spot opportunities.

Gen Z Sales Hack: Be Real, Not Perfect

Gen Z can sniff out inauthenticity from a mile away. They don't want polished, corporate-speaking posts; they want realness. Share your wins *and* your struggles. Talk about the lessons you've learned. Post behind-the-scenes moments that show you're human.

- Example: A freelance designer posted a raw Instagram story about a client ghosting her after she delivered a project. She turned it into a teachable moment about setting boundaries. Not only did the story resonate with her audience, but she also got three new inquiries from people who admired her honesty.

The Bottom Line

Social selling isn't about selling, it's about connecting. Whether you're sliding into LinkedIn messages or hopping on TikTok trends, the key is authenticity. Share values, start conversations, and build relationships.

The sales world is shifting to digital, and the best sellers aren't just keeping up—they're thriving.

4. B2B Sales Meets eCommerce: The Game Has Changed

Forget everything you thought you knew about B2B sales. It's no longer about handshakes over lunch or marathon meetings with decision-makers flipping through bulky catalogs. Today, B2B sales are looking a lot more like B2C. Why? Because the new generation of buyers doesn't want outdated processes—they want convenience, speed, and seamless online experiences.

The numbers don't lie:

- 70% of B2B buyers are willing to spend up to $500,000 on a single eCommerce transaction.
- 83% of buyers are open to dropping over $10 million online.

B2B eCommerce is exploding, and if you're not adapting, you're falling behind. Let's explore how these changes are reshaping the sales game and what you can do to stay ahead.

Why B2B is Going Digital

Think about it: Today's B2B buyers are the same people who shop on Amazon and stream Netflix. They expect the same level of convenience in their professional lives as they do at home. The rise of digital platforms, self-service portals, and subscription models isn't just a trend—it's the new standard.

Sales teams are no longer just order-takers; they're becoming strategic advisors. Their job? Guiding clients through big, complex purchases while letting digital tools handle the straightforward stuff.

Real World Story: The $1 Million Click

Imagine this: A procurement manager for a global manufacturing company needs $1 million worth of industrial equipment. Instead of calling a sales rep, they log onto an eCommerce portal, compare options, and complete the purchase—all in a single afternoon.

This isn't the future. It's happening right now. Platforms like Alibaba and industry-specific marketplaces are enabling massive B2B transactions online. Companies investing in these tools are winning big, while others scramble to catch up.

Lesson: Buyers want control. Give them tools to self-serve when it makes sense and focus your sales team on adding value where it matters most.

CHAPTER 3

The 4-Legged Stool of Value Proposition: A Modern Framework for Sales Excellence

In today's world, where customer expectations shift at lightning speed and new trends redefine the marketplace, a strong value proposition is no longer optional—it's essential. But a winning value proposition isn't just about solving today's problems. It's about continuously evolving to meet tomorrow's challenges while delivering relevance, unforgettable experiences, trust, and adaptability.

This isn't just a theory. It's a strategy that transforms how you connect with buyers in both digital and real-world settings.

The Four Legs of the Value Proposition Stool

1. **Relevance**: Speak to what matters most to the buyer right now.
2. **Experience**: Create moments that go beyond expectations and leave lasting impressions.
3. **Trust**: Build unwavering confidence through authenticity, transparency, and proof.
4. **Adaptability**: Stay flexible and evolve with the buyer's needs and the changing market.

When these four legs are balanced, your value proposition stands strong. Let's explore each pillar through modern insights and relatable examples.

1. Relevance: Solve What Matters Most Right Now

Today's buyers expect you to know their challenges before they tell you. Especially Gen Z, who demand solutions that are hyper-personalized, align with their values, and address their current priorities.

How to Achieve Relevance:

- **Hyper-Personalization**: Use tools like AI to craft tailored messaging.
  - *Example*: A fitness app recommends custom workout plans based on a user's recent searches and fitness goals.
- **Value-Driven Messaging**: Highlight ethical practices, sustainability, or other shared values.
  - *Example*: A clothing brand emphasizes its eco-friendly materials when pitching to environmentally conscious shoppers.
- **Real-Time Relevance**: Respond to current trends or events.

o   *Example*: A cybersecurity firm positions its solution as urgent after a high-profile industry data breach.

Why It Matters:

Relevance grabs attention in a world full of noise. When buyers feel like your offer speaks directly to their needs, they're far more likely to engage.

2. **Experience: Deliver Beyond Expectations**

Buyers don't just buy products—they buy how those products make them feel. A great experience isn't a bonus; it's a necessity. For Gen Z, who prioritize experiences over material possessions, this leg of the stool is critical.

How to Deliver Memorable Experiences:

- **Interactive Touchpoints**: Let buyers engage with your product in creative ways.
  - o   *Example*: A real estate agent uses AR/VR technology to let clients virtually tour homes.
- **Delightful Surprises**: Add unexpected value.
  - o   *Example*: A café includes a personalized note with each order, creating a personal connection.
- **Seamless Journeys**: Remove friction at every step.
  - o   *Example*: An e-commerce site offers one-click checkout and free returns.

Why It Matters:

An exceptional experience builds loyalty and turns buyers into advocates. People may forget what you sold them, but they'll never forget how you made them feel.

3. **Trust: Build Unshakable Confidence**

Modern buyers are naturally skeptical. They've seen overpromises, hidden fees, and too-good-to-be-true pitches. Trust bridges the gap between interest and action.

How to Build Trust:

- **Transparency**: Be upfront about pricing, timelines, and challenges.
  - o *Example*: A SaaS company provides clear, straightforward pricing with no hidden fees.
- **Social Proof**: Show testimonials, reviews, and case studies.
  - o *Example*: A fitness brand posts video testimonials of customers sharing their transformation stories.
- **Authentic Relationships**: Be genuine and empathetic.
  - o *Example*: A salesperson remembers personal details, like a prospect's recent milestone, and incorporates it into follow-ups.

Why It Matters:

Trust removes hesitation. Buyers who trust you won't just make one purchase; they'll return, recommend you to others, and become lifelong advocates.

4. **Adaptability: Evolve with the Buyer and the Market**

The only constant in today's sales world is change. Buyers' needs evolve, technologies advance, and market dynamics shift. Adaptability ensures your value proposition remains relevant no matter what.

How to Stay Adaptable:

- **Respond to Market Changes**: Adjust your pitch or offering based on external events.
  o *Example*: A hotel introduces remote work packages during the pandemic to cater to changing customer needs.
- **Embrace New Platforms**: Meet buyers where they are—whether that's TikTok, Discord, or emerging spaces.
  o *Example*: A fashion brand launches exclusive collections on TikTok Shop, tapping into Gen Z's preferred platform.
- **Continuous Learning**: Use feedback to refine your approach.
  o *Example*: A customer service team analyzes surveys to identify and resolve pain points.
- **Real-Time Adjustments**: Adapt during live interactions based on buyer responses.
  o *Example*: A car salesperson shifts their pitch mid-conversation to focus on features the buyer expresses interest in.

Why It Matters:

Adaptability ensures longevity. It shows buyers that you're not just offering a solution for today—you're ready to grow with them into the future.

How the Four Legs Work Together

Think of Nike. They exemplify the 4-legged stool in action:

a. **Relevance**: Nike connects with Gen Z by promoting inclusivity and sustainability, aligning with their values.
b. **Experience**: The Nike app offers personalized workouts, exclusive product drops, and seamless navigation.
c. **Trust**: Transparent sourcing and endorsements from top athletes build confidence in their products.

d. **Adaptability**: Nike adapts to cultural trends, launching collaborations with influencers and creating campaigns that resonate with younger audiences.

Why the 4-Legged Stool Is Essential

In today's fast-paced sales landscape:

- **Relevance** ensures your offer gets noticed.
- **Experience** makes buyers want to stay.
- **Trust** gives them the confidence to commit.
- **Adaptability** keeps you ahead of the curve.

Without all four legs, your value proposition wobbles:

- Without Relevance, your offer feels out of touch.
- Without Experience, buyers may come once but won't return.
- Without Trust, skepticism will block conversions.
- Without Adaptability, you risk irrelevance as trends and needs evolve.

Imagine walking into a store where the salesperson immediately knows what you're looking for (Relevance), offers to let you try it out in a fun and engaging way (Experience), shares stories of how others loved it (Trust), and adjusts their pitch when you mention a specific need (Adaptability). That's what Gen Z craves—a sales experience that feels personal, seamless, and future-ready.

Interactive Exercise: Build Your 4-Legged Stool

For Each Leg, Ask Yourself:

1. **Relevance**: What problem am I solving right now? How does this align with my buyer's goals?

2. **Experience**: How can I make this interaction enjoyable, memorable, and frictionless?
3. **Trust**: What proof or transparency can I offer to make my buyer feel confident?
4. **Adaptability**: How can I evolve my approach based on buyer feedback or market shifts?

The 4-legged stool of Relevance, Experience, Trust, and Adaptability is more than a theory—it's your roadmap for connecting with buyers on every level. In a world of endless options, it's how you stay not just in the game, but ahead of it.

While a strong value proposition ensures a solid foundation for sales success, the way you engage with buyers also plays a critical role. It's not just about providing quick fixes—it's about empowering customers with the right tools and knowledge to make informed decisions. This brings us to the next key distinction in modern sales: helping vs. enabling.

Helping vs. Enabling: The New Playbook for Sales in a Digital World

*Imagine this: You're knee-deep in assembling IKEA furniture. Someone hands you a screwdriver. That's **helping**—a quick fix to get you through. But what if they go a step further? What if they not only give you the screwdriver but also provide a step-by-step tutorial, pre-sort the pieces, and even throw in an AI assistant to alert you before you misalign a screw? That's **enabling**—empowering you not just to finish this one project but to master furniture assembly forever.*

*In sales, **helping** is solving problems in the moment, while **enabling** is building systems that empower teams to succeed consistently. Gen Z—a generation that values independence and tools to thrive—wants sales interactions that feel like enabling, not just helping. Let's break it down.*

What Does Enabling Sales Look Like?

Sales enablement isn't just a buzzword; it's the foundation of lasting success. It's about arming sales teams with the right tools, insights, and confidence to tackle challenges proactively. Think of it as creating an ecosystem where reps don't just sell, they thrive.

How AI Transforms Enabling Sales

AI isn't just the sidekick of sales—it's the superhero. By automating repetitive tasks, analyzing complex data, and offering real-time insights, AI shifts sales from reactive to strategic, from firefighting to forward-thinking.

1. *AI-Driven Insights: From Guesswork to Precision*

   - *The Old Way (Helping): A manager tells a rep, "Focus on this lead. It looks promising," based on gut instinct.*
   - *The New Way (Enabling): AI crunches customer behavior, purchase history, and engagement metrics to deliver a ranked list of leads most likely to convert.*

Picture a real estate agency that used to rely on instinct to prioritize leads. With AI, they now analyze market trends to identify entire neighborhoods with rising demand. Reps don't just chase one hot lead—they create targeted strategies for high-potential areas. AI isn't just helping them sell; it's enabling them to dominate.

2. *Automating the Grind: Focus on What Matters*

   - *The Old Way (Helping): An assistant spends hours manually updating CRM notes after every meeting.*
   - *The New Way (Enabling): AI tools like Gong or Salesforce Einstein automatically capture and organize meeting notes, freeing reps to focus on what they do best: building relationships.*

A SaaS sales team used to spend up to two hours a day logging calls and emails into their CRM. Today, AI handles all of it instantly. Those two hours are now spent engaging customers, resulting in a 25% increase in closed deals. That's not just efficiency, it's empowerment.

3. **Personalized Sales Journeys: Magic in the Moment**

- **The Old Way (Helping):** *A rep guesses which features to emphasize during a demo, hoping they hit the right chord.*
- **The New Way (Enabling):** *AI tracks customer behavior in real time and suggests the most relevant features, case studies, and pricing models.*

At a luxury car dealership, AI tracks a buyer's clicks on the website, showroom visits, and past conversations with reps. The system flags that the customer is most interested in custom interiors and fuel efficiency. The rep walks into the meeting armed with exactly what the customer wants to hear. The deal closes faster than ever—because it felt tailor-made.

4. **Proactive Customer Support: Solving Problems Before They Happen**

- **The Old Way (Helping):** *A customer calls with an issue, and a rep fixes it.*
- **The New Way (Enabling):** *AI monitors product usage and flags potential issues before they escalate, empowering reps to proactively engage customers.*

A fitness app notices when users stop logging workouts and sends personalized tips to re-engage them. One user, who felt overwhelmed by advanced workouts, gets a "Beginner's Challenge" tailored just for them. Not only does the user stay subscribed, but they also share their journey on social media, bringing in new customers. That's AI turning churn into cheer.

Why Enabling Sales Resonates with Gen Z

Gen Z buyers want to feel like they're in control. They despise pushy salespeople and value empowerment over handholding. To win them over, sales teams must offer tools, resources, and insights that let them steer their own journey.

A Gen Z video creator is exploring video editing software. Instead of being bombarded with a features pitch, they get an AI-powered onboarding process. Tutorials, sample projects, and personalized recommendations show them exactly how the software can make their TikTok go viral. By the time the sales team follows up, they're not selling—they're celebrating.

Helping vs. Enabling: Spot the Difference

Helping Sales	*Enabling Sales*
Reacts to problems as they arise	*Anticipates and prevents issues*
Focuses on one deal at a time	*Builds systems for repeatable success*
Relies on gut instinct	*Leverages data and AI-driven insights*
Fixes symptoms	*Addresses root causes*

Big Thought: Build Systems, Not Shortcuts

Helping sales is like putting a band-aid on a cut—it works in the moment but doesn't prevent the next one. Enabling sales is like teaching someone to take care of their health, it builds a foundation for lasting success. In today's digital world, AI is the ultimate enabler, turning data into action and challenges into opportunities.

"Helping is a momentary fix. Enabling is a movement. In sales, the future belongs to those who don't just close deals but empower their teams and customers to thrive."

Mute Button and Allies

In sales, sometimes it's luck that steps in to help; other times, it's the people around you. And then there are those unexpected moments that shape the deal in ways you'd never have predicted. In this next story, you'll see how the simple press—or rather, *non-press*—of the mute button closed the sale.

Sales and negotiations often involve forces outside your control that work in your favor, shifting the balance just when you need it. This story is one of those rare moments. A sales rep was in the middle of intense negotiations with a company, juggling a call that involved both the operations and procurement teams. At one point, the company asked the rep to hold for a few minutes so they could discuss his offer internally.

But there was one detail they forgot: to hit the mute button.

As the sales rep waited, he could clearly hear the conversation unfolding on the other end. He listened as the operations and procurement teams discussed his product's perfect fit for their needs, revealing just how indispensable it had become to their business. He realized exactly what they needed and how his offer aligned with their requirements. With this insider insight, he knew he was closer than ever to sealing the deal.

And sure enough, the deal closed. Sometimes, the best sales tools aren't strategies or pitches—they're the happy accidents that tip the scale your way.

Another powerful example comes from Daymond John, founder and CEO of the hip-hop clothing brand FUBU. He often credits his mother and friends for his success. His mother, who taught him how to sew, believed in his dream so strongly that she took a second mortgage on their house to support his venture. And his friends from the neighborhood backed him by wearing and promoting his clothes. John's story carries a valuable lesson: if you can't convince the people closest to you to believe in your ideas and support your products, who else will?

Whether it's luck, the mute button, or the unwavering support of those around you, sales is often about finding your allies—those who see the value in what you're offering and believe in it as much as you do.

CHAPTER 4

From the Right Bus to the Whole Journey: The Evolution of Sales Thinking

Imagine you're about to embark on a road trip. At first, the only thing that seems to matter is picking the right bus and knowing where you're going. It's all about reaching the destination as fast as possible. But then, you start thinking about the people you're traveling with. Are they the right companions? Do they make the ride enjoyable? Finally, it hits you, the most memorable part of the journey isn't just arriving at the destination; it's the experiences along the way.

This shift—from focusing on the bus to the passengers, to the journey itself—captures the evolution of sales. It's not just a metaphor; it's a reflection of how businesses have adapted to meet customer expectations, create value, and deliver experiences that resonate with modern buyers, especially Gen Z.

The First Era: The Right Bus to the Right Destination

In the early days of sales, everything was about efficiency and results. Think of this era like running a bus service—businesses focused on picking the right vehicle (product or service) and mapping the fastest route to the destination (profit). The destination was clear: sell as much as possible to as many people as possible.

For example, imagine a soda company in the 1950s. Their entire strategy revolved around getting their product into stores, no questions asked. Advertising was one-size-fits-all, plastered across billboards and magazines. Salespeople were measured by how many crates of soda they could push to distributors. It didn't matter if customers felt connected to the brand or if the product added value to their lives—the goal was to get the soda on shelves and into hands.

At this stage, sales were transactional, impersonal, and all about the bottom line. Customers were treated like passengers hopping on a bus to get somewhere, not as individuals with unique needs or preferences.

The Second Era: Finding the Right People on the Bus

As markets grew competitive and customers became more discerning, businesses realized that the product alone wasn't enough. They needed to put the right people on the bus—customers who not only bought the product but resonated with the brand's vision. This era was about connection.

Let's go forward to the 1990s, when companies like Nike changed the game. Nike wasn't just selling sneakers; they were selling a lifestyle. Their marketing focused on empowering individuals to "just do it." Suddenly, it wasn't about pushing products; it was about building a community. They sought the right customers—people who wanted to feel like athletes, dreamers, and doers.

Sales strategies adapted, too. Personalization became the name of the game. Businesses started using customer data to tailor their approaches. They asked questions: *Who is our ideal customer? What do they value? How can we meet them where they are?*

At this point, sales became less about reaching a destination and more about understanding the passengers. It was about making sure the right people were on the journey with you, building loyalty and trust along the way.

The Third Era: The Whole Journey

Now, we've arrived at the present day, where the focus has shifted yet again. It's no longer just about the bus or even the passengers, it's about the entire experience of the journey. Why? Because customers don't just want products; they want experiences that add value to their lives.

Take Spotify as an example. Spotify doesn't just sell music; it creates a personal soundtrack for your life. With AI-driven playlists like "Discover Weekly," Spotify anticipates your taste and evolves with you. The journey doesn't end when you subscribe—it continues as Spotify learns your preferences, recommends new songs, and even creates playlists for every mood.

In the sales world, this means businesses are no longer just closing deals; they're building ongoing relationships. It's about crafting a seamless, meaningful experience from the first touchpoint to long after the sale. For example, when you buy an iPhone, Apple doesn't stop at the sale. They've designed every moment—from unboxing to setup to customer support—to feel effortless and engaging.

This focus on the journey reflects a deeper understanding of value. Customers don't measure satisfaction by whether they reach the destination but by *how* they got there. The journey becomes the product, and the experience becomes the brand.

Why This Evolution Matters for Gen Z

Gen Z, this story is about you. Your generation grew up with unlimited choices and instant access to information. You don't settle for good enough—you expect the best. You're not just looking for products; you're looking for brands that align with your values, create memorable experiences, and treat you like an individual.

For you, sales isn't about being sold to. It's about feeling understood. It's about brands creating value for you before, during, and after the transaction. And when they do, you reward them with your loyalty— and your influence.

Lessons from the Journey

1. **The Bus (Product) Still Matters, but It's Not Enough:** The foundation of any sales process is a great product or service. But customers today want more than functionality—they want a brand that resonates with them emotionally.
2. **The People (Customers) Are Everything:** Understanding your audience is critical. This means listening, adapting, and building trust through meaningful interactions.

3. **The Journey Is the New Destination:** The most successful sales strategies focus on creating an experience that adds value at every step. This is where magic happens.

The Takeaway: Make the Journey Count

Sales today isn't just about what you sell, it's about how you make people feel. The destination might still matter, but the journey is where relationships are built, loyalty is earned, and value is created.

For Gen Z, this is the new reality. Whether you're selling sneakers, software, or ideas, remember: It's not just about getting customers on the bus—it's about making sure the ride is unforgettable.

Selling to the Limitless Generation: Redefining Sales in the Digital Age

Welcome to the New World of Sales

Sales isn't just a numbers game anymore; it's a *people game*. And the rules have changed. Today, your customers aren't just looking for a product; they're looking for meaning, speed, and a seamless, authentic experience. Gen Z, the first fully digital generation, doesn't just want brands; they want brands that stand for something.

This book is your guide to mastering sales in a world without limits. It's not just about mastering tactics; it's about speaking the language of the limitless generation. We'll explore how to integrate classic marketing theories into a digital-first sales approach and teach you how to make sales relevant to Gen Z. Ready to adapt, evolve, and connect with your most important customers yet? Let's go.

Marketing Myopia—Why You're Looking in the Wrong Direction

Marketing Myopia, the timeless concept from Theodore Levitt, warned companies about being too product-focused instead of customer-focused. In today's world, this concept is more critical than ever. If you're only selling *what* your product does and not *why* it matters, you've already lost the game.

What Gen Z Expects

1. **Purpose Over Product:** Gen Z doesn't just want a soft drink; they want a company that supports environmental sustainability. It's not about the features anymore; it's about the story.
2. **Relatability Over Rigidity:** Forget corporate jargon. Speak in memes, emojis, and real-world language. Gen Z values brands that feel human.

Applying Marketing Myopia to Sales

- Don't sell shoes; sell self-expression, sustainability, and freedom to move.
- Don't pitch tech gadgets; pitch convenience, status, and the empowerment they bring.

Practical Tip: Create narratives around your product. Use storytelling to make the customer the hero and your product the sidekick that solves their problem.

Gen Z—The Limitless Generation

Gen Z is unlike any customer base you've encountered before. Born into the digital age, they live in a world of endless options, limitless access to information, and instant gratification.

Key Characteristics of Gen Z:

- **They Value Authenticity:** They'll sniff out a fake pitch in seconds. If you're not genuine, you're irrelevant.
- **They're Community-Driven:** They don't just follow brands—they build tribes around them.
- **They Crave Speed:** A delayed response to a DM? Lost sale.

How to Speak Gen Z's Language in Sales

1. **Social First:** If your brand isn't active on TikTok or Instagram, Gen Z won't even know you exist. Leverage short-form content, user-generated posts, and viral trends.
2. **Collaborate With Influencers:** They trust influencers more than traditional ads. Build relationships with creators who align with your brand values.
3. **Interactive Sales Techniques:** Use polls, quizzes, and live Q&A sessions to create engaging experiences. Gen Z doesn't want to be talked *at*—they want to be involved.

Sales Techniques That Actually Work for Gen Z

Gone are the days of cold calls and scripted pitches. Today's sales techniques must be innovative, personalized, and interactive.

1. Personalization at Scale

Gen Z expects you to know who they are and what they want—before they even tell you. Leverage AI to anticipate their needs:

- Use browsing history and past purchases to recommend products.
- Send hyper-personalized follow-up emails that speak directly to their preferences.

2. Social Selling

Forget email campaigns. Gen Z lives on social media. Your Instagram DMs and TikTok comments section are the new sales floor:

- Respond to comments in real time.
- Use Stories and Reels to showcase your product in action.
- Partner with micro-influencers for authentic product recommendations.

3. Interactive Sales

Engage your customers with gamification:

- Host quizzes to recommend products based on their personality.
- Create challenges and contests that encourage them to showcase how they use your product.

The ZHUZH Sales Technique

The term **zhuzh** (pronounced "zhuzh" or "zhoozh") is often used in informal English and means: **To make something more interesting, attractive, or stylish, especially by adding a small amount of effort or embellishment.**

Let's face it: traditional sales techniques can feel as dusty as a VHS tape in a Netflix world. The Gen Z marketplace is a vibe—a colorful, dynamic ecosystem driven by connection, creativity, and authenticity. Herr I reiterate that Selling isn't just about closing deals anymore; it's about standing out, creating value, and staying unforgettable.

That's where *ZHUZH* comes in. It's not just a technique, it's an attitude, a philosophy, and your secret weapon for mastering sales in today's world.

What Is ZHUZH?

At its core, ZHUZH is about taking something ordinary and elevating it to extraordinary. It's the flair, the sparkle, the added energy that turns a simple pitch into a story, a product into an experience, and a customer into a loyal advocate.

Here's what ZHUZH stands for:

1. **Z** - *Zone In on Their World*
2. **H** - *Humanize the Connection*
3. **U** - *Unlock Unexpected Value*
4. **Z** - *Zero in on Collaboration*
5. **H** - *Highlight Their Win*

Breaking Down ZHUZH

1. **Zone In on Their World**

Stop selling. Start observing. Who is your customer? What do they care about? Gen Z, Millennials, or even Gen Alpha aren't looking for generic solutions—they want hyper-personalized experiences.

- **Example**: A customer posts on TikTok about their love for eco-friendly products. When pitching your product, don't just highlight its features—connect it to their values. "This isn't just another water bottle; it's your statement against plastic waste."

Tip: Do your homework. Social media stalking (the ethical kind!) isn't creepy, it's insightful.

2. Humanize the Connection

People buy from people, not robots. Bring personality into the conversation. Be real, relatable, and a little vulnerable.

- **Example**: Instead of a scripted cold email, send a voice note or video message. Say, "Hey, I saw you're growing your startup, and I've been there too. Here's how I think we can help."

Tip: Use humor, share anecdotes, or show genuine excitement—it makes you unforgettable.

3. Unlock Unexpected Value

This is where you zhuzh it up. Go beyond what's expected. Surprise them with values they didn't even know they needed.

- **Example**: You're pitching a social media management tool. Instead of just listing its features, offer a free insights into their current engagement status. "Hey, I noticed your posts peak at 7 PM—let's amplify that with our tool."

Tip: Always ask, "What's one thing I can give that will blow their mind today?"

4. **Zero in on Collaboration**

Gen Z thrives on partnerships, co-creation, and a sense of ownership. Your product isn't just something they buy; it's something they're a part of.

- **Example**: Pitch your SaaS platform not as a service, but as a partnership. "We don't just offer tools; we'll build a custom roadmap with you to ensure success."

Tip: Use words like "we," "together," and "build." Make it about them, not you.

5. **Highlight Their Win**

Forget hard selling—celebrate their success instead. Show how your product or service doesn't just fit into their world but transforms it.

- **Example**: After a trial period, follow up with, "Here's how your engagement increased by 40% this month—imagine what we could do long-term."

Tip: Make your client the hero of the story. You're just the guide helping them achieve greatness.

Why ZHUZH Works in Today's Sales World

- **It's Human:** Gen Z and Millennials crave authenticity. They don't want polished scripts, they want raw, real connections.
- **It's Unexpected:** In a world of generic pitches, ZHUZH makes you stand out. It's not about what you're selling, it's about how you make them feel.

- **It's Value-Driven:** ZHUZH isn't about closing quick deals; it's about creating long-term relationships. And relationships? That's where the real magic happens.

Let's take the ZHUZH technique and apply it to real estate—whether you're selling residential homes, commercial spaces, or investment properties. The competitive landscape of real estate is perfect for this value-driven, creative approach.

Scenario: Selling a Suburban Family Home

1. Zone In on Their World

Understand the buyer's needs, values, and lifestyle. Who are they? A young family, perhaps, looking for a safe neighborhood, good schools, and a space to grow?

Example:

Before the showing, research the family. Notice they have kids? Create a personalized experience:

- Provide a neighborhood guide highlighting nearby parks, schools, and kid-friendly activities.
- Share photos of local community events to emphasize the welcoming vibe.

"Hey, I noticed you have two young kids. I think you'll love the playground just two blocks away—it's a favorite for local families.

2. Humanize the Connection

Make the interaction personal and authentic. Don't just walk them through the house; tell a story about how it fits their life.

Example:

Instead of saying, "This is the living room," say:

"Can't you just picture movie nights here with the family? Add some popcorn and cozy blankets, and this space will become your go-to spot for memories.

Pro Tip: Share your own connection to the area, like, "I live a mile from here, and my favorite part is how quiet it gets at night—perfect for a good night's sleep."

3. **Unlock Unexpected Value**

Offer something beyond the house itself. Surprise them with additional insights or perks.

Example:

- Provide free consultation with a local interior designer to help them envision the space.
- Create a digital mock-up of how the backyard could look with a garden or a play area for the kids.

"Here's a 3D layout we made that shows how you could easily add a play area here. It'd be a perfect space for the kids to burn off some energy while you relax."

4. **Zero in on Collaboration**

Frame the process as a partnership, not just a sale. Be their guide, not just their agent.

Example:

"You mentioned you're worried about moving during the school year. Let's work together to find a timeline that keeps things smooth for your family. I can also introduce you to my favorite local movers—they're amazing with families."

Pro Tip: If they're unsure about financing, connect them with trusted mortgage advisors and make introductions on their behalf.

5. **Highlight Their Win**

Celebrate how this home fits their dream, and show measurable benefits like affordability, growth potential, or lifestyle improvements.

Example:

"When we first spoke, you said you wanted a home where the kids could grow up safely, close to good schools. This neighborhood's school district ranks in the top 5 in the state, and homes here typically increase in value by 10% every year—this isn't just a home; it's an investment in your family's future."

Result of ZHUZH in Real Estate

By applying ZHUZH, you don't just sell a house—you create an experience:

- **The family feels understood** because you've zoned in on their needs.
- **They trust you** because you've humanized the process and offered genuine advice.
- **They see value** in the personalized extras you've provided.
- • **They feel like partners** in the process, not passive buyers.

- **They know their win** and how this decision benefits them in the short and long term.

In real estate, it's not just about the property, it's about the lifestyle, the connection, and the vision you create for your clients. ZHUZH transforms the way you sell by making every interaction an experience, every pitch a story, and every deal a partnership.

Because in the end, you're not just helping them buy a home, you're helping them build a life. And that's the ultimate ZHUZH.

From the Funnel to the Flywheel—A New Sales Model

The traditional sales funnel is obsolete. Gen Z doesn't follow a straight line from awareness to purchase. They loop, revisit, and engage at multiple touchpoints. Enter the **Flywheel Model**:

- **Attract:** Use social media, influencers, and content marketing to bring them in.
- **Engage:** Keep them hooked with interactive experiences and personalized recommendations.
- **Delight:** Follow up with stellar customer service and surprises (like free gifts or shout-outs on social media).

Practical Tip: Turn your satisfied customers into your best salespeople. Gen Z loves to share reviews, post unboxing videos, and tag brands they love.

The Power of Marketing Theories in Sales

Sales isn't just about charisma—it's about strategy. Here's how classic marketing theories can revolutionize your sales game:

1. **Marketing Myopia Revisited**

Stop thinking about products in isolation. Instead, think about the lifestyle, identity, or emotional need your product fulfills.

2. **The 4Ps Reimagined**

- **Product:** It's not what you sell; it's how it fits into their world.
- **Price:** Value matters more than cost. How does your price align with their values?
- **Place:** Be everywhere they are, from Instagram to their favorite local coffee shop.
- **Promotion:** Memes, influencers, and stories > ads.

3. **The Decision-Making Journey**

Understand that Gen Z doesn't just buy; they research, evaluate, and compare endlessly. Your job? Be present at every stage:

- Awareness: Create viral content that stops their scroll.
- Consideration: Share testimonials, user stories, and behind-the-scenes content.
- Decision: Offer seamless checkout options and limited-time incentives.

Embracing Technology in Sales

Technology isn't replacing salespeople; it's empowering them. Here's how to leverage it:

- **AI for Lead Generation:** Predict which customers are most likely to buy.
- **Chatbots for Instant Engagement:** Provide instant answers 24/7.
- **Data-Driven Insights:** Use analytics to refine your approach and improve your conversion rates.

Gen Z Wants More Than Products—They Want Purpose

For Gen Z, a brand's ethics matter as much as its products. They're buying into what you stand for.

How to Sell with Purpose

1. **Be Transparent:** Show them where your materials come from, how your products are made, and how you treat your employees.
2. **Take a Stand:** Align with causes that matter to your audience, whether it's sustainability, diversity, or mental health awareness.
3. **Celebrate Community:** Create opportunities for your customers to connect, share, and collaborate.
4. Selling to Gen Z isn't just about mastering the latest tools or trends. It's about understanding their values, meeting them where they are, and creating genuine connections. This limitless generation isn't just transforming sales, they're transforming the way we think about business.

If you can adapt, evolve, and embrace this new world, the opportunities are endless. Are you ready to sell without limits? Let's make it happen.

CHAPTER 5

Introducing the S.A.L.E.S. Theory: Selling to the Limitless Generation

Modern sales require more than just a strong pitch—it demands a structured yet adaptable approach that aligns with today's digital-first, experience-driven world. To navigate this landscape, I've developed the **S.A.L.E.S. Theory**, a framework designed to help sales professionals connect with and convert the limitless generation of buyers.

In this section, we'll break down each component of the **S.A.L.E.S. Theory** and explore how you can apply its principles effectively. With real-world examples and actionable strategies, this framework will equip you with the tools to build meaningful relationships, drive engagement, and sustain long-term success in an ever-evolving market.

S - Setting Goals and Strategy

Setting clear, actionable, and customer-focused goals is the foundation of modern sales. However, these goals must now align with the customer's journey, preferences, and digital habits.

How to Implement:

Define SMART Goals:

Specific: Understand what success looks like for the customer (e.g., helping them save time or live healthier).

Measurable: Track KPIs such as engagement rates, conversion rates, and customer satisfaction.

Achievable: Break down ambitious goals into actionable steps.

Relevant: Ensure your goals align with your company's values and the customer's needs.

Time-Bound: Set timelines to deliver results efficiently.

Align Your Goals with Customer Goals:

Example: Instead of focusing on selling a fitness tracker, aim to help customers meet their wellness targets by creating personalized workout programs and tracking tools.

Case Example:

Nike's Goals with Gen Z: Nike doesn't just aim to sell sneakers; it aims to inspire a global community of athletes, regardless of skill level. Through the Nike Training Club App, they set a goal to help users stay active during the pandemic by offering free premium workouts. This aligned with their customers' need for health and well-being, creating loyalty and boosting app downloads.

A - Adapting to the Digital Customer

The modern customer is not just digital; they are omnichannel, informed, and demanding. They expect brands to be everywhere they are—and they demand instant, personalized service.

How to Implement:

Be Omnichannel:

Maintain a consistent brand presence across platforms like Instagram, TikTok, YouTube, and even gaming platforms.

Adapt your tone to each platform: Professional on LinkedIn, playful on TikTok.

Leverage AI and Automation:

Use AI-powered tools like chatbots to provide real-time responses.

Employ predictive analytics to recommend products based on browsing behavior.

Meet Customers Where They Are:

Example: If your target audience spends hours scrolling TikTok, create bite-sized, engaging videos that highlight your product's benefits in a relatable way.

L - Listening and Learning

Listening is no longer just a skill; it's a superpower. In today's world, it's about gathering insights not only through conversations but also by analyzing data, social media trends, and customer behavior.

How to Implement:

Social Listening:

Use tools like Brandwatch or Sprout Social to monitor mentions of your brand, competitors, and industry trends.

Identify recurring pain points or unmet needs through customer reviews and online comments.

Learn From Data:

Use analytics platforms like Google Analytics or Shopify Insights to track customer behavior on your website.

Use heatmaps to identify where customers spend the most time and optimize those sections.

Ask for Feedback:

Example: Send post-purchase surveys asking how customers have found their experience and what you can improve.

Case Example:

Spotify's Playlist Personalization: Spotify listens to its users' preferences through data. By analyzing listening habits, they create personalized playlists like "Discover Weekly," which keeps users engaged and coming back.

E - Engaging Through Experiences

Selling is no longer just about pitching a product; it's about creating memorable experiences that customers want to share. Engagement is the currency of trust and loyalty.

How to Implement:

Create Interactive Experiences:

Use augmented reality (AR) to let customers "try before they buy." For example, IKEA's AR app allows customers to visualize how furniture will look in their homes.

Host live events or webinars to interact directly with your audience.

Gamify the Process:

Offer rewards for engaging actions, like completing surveys or sharing a product on social media.

Example: Starbucks' loyalty program uses gamification to reward frequent customers with stars they can redeem for free drinks.

Involve Your Audience:

Create campaigns that encourage user-generated content (UGC). For example, ask customers to share their stories using your product with a branded hashtag.

Case Example:

Coca-Cola's "Share a Coke": This campaign engaged customers by personalizing bottles with names, encouraging them to share photos on social media. The result? Massive global engagement and an emotional connection with the brand.

S - Sustaining Relationships

The sales process doesn't end at the transaction—it begins there. Sustaining relationships turns one-time buyers into lifelong advocates.

How to Implement:

Build Community:

Create exclusive online groups where customers can connect and share experiences.

Example: Lululemon's ambassador program builds a community around its brand.

Provide Exceptional After-Sales Service:

Offer free tutorials, resources, or webinars to help customers get the most out of their purchases.

Example: A tech company could provide free online workshops on how to use their software effectively.

Reward Loyalty:

Develop tiered loyalty programs that offer increasing benefits for repeat customers.

Examples: Sephora's Beauty Insider program offers points, early access to sales, and exclusive events.

Amazon Prime: Amazon sustains customer relationships by providing ongoing value through fast shipping, exclusive content, and discounts, creating a sense of belonging and trust.

Bringing S.A.L.E.S. Together With an Example

Imagine you're selling eco-friendly water bottles targeting Gen Z:

S - Setting Goals: Instead of just selling bottles, your goal is to help reduce single-use plastic consumption by 1 million bottles in the next year.

A - Adapting: You create TikTok campaigns with influencers demonstrating how the bottle fits into a sustainable lifestyle.

L - Listening: You monitor comments to learn that customers want bottles in pastel colors and act quickly to produce them.

E - Engaging: You launch an AR Instagram filter where users can "customize" their bottles and share it with friends.

S - Sustaining: You send personalized thank-you notes with tips on how to clean and care for the bottle, along with a discount code for their next purchase.

Conclusion

The S.A.L.E.S. Theory isn't just a sales strategy; it's a complete transformation of how businesses approach customers in the digital age. By setting clear goals, adapting to digital behaviors, listening to your audience, creating engaging experiences, and sustaining relationships, you're not just selling—you're building lasting connections in a limitless world.

With this framework, you'll speak the language of Gen Z, deliver unparalleled value, and thrive in the ever-changing sales landscape. Now, let's take these principles and redefine what it means to sell in the digital era.

The Dream 100 Reimagined and Education-Based Marketing in the Digital Era

In the traditional sales world, Chet Holmes' *Dream 100* strategy revolutionized how businesses approached their most valuable prospects. Instead of scattering efforts across hundreds or thousands of leads, Holmes advised salespeople to focus their energy on a carefully selected list of 100 ideal clients—those who would provide the greatest return on investment. It's a concept rooted in laser-focused effort, consistency, and persistence.

But the digital era has transformed how we identify, reach, and nurture these "Dream 100" prospects. With tools like AI and social media platforms such as TikTok and YouTube, the modern salesperson has the ability to make this classic strategy more powerful than ever before.

The Modern Dream 100: Powered by AI

In the past, identifying a Dream 100 list relied heavily on manual research, intuition, and relationship-building. Today, **AI has revolutionized this process**, making it faster, more accurate, and scalable.

How AI Identifies Your Dream 100

1. **Data-Driven Prospecting:** AI tools analyze massive datasets from customer behaviors, industry trends, and competitor

activities to identify your ideal prospects. Platforms like HubSpot, Salesforce, and LinkedIn Sales Navigator use algorithms to pinpoint businesses or individuals who are most likely to convert.

    o **Example:** Instead of manually searching for high-value accounts, an AI tool might identify the top 100 companies in your target market based on factors like revenue, social media engagement, or website visits.

2. **Predictive Analytics:** AI doesn't just help find potential customers; it predicts which ones are most likely to buy. By analyzing historical data, AI can rank prospects based on their likelihood to respond to your sales pitch or convert into long-term clients.

    o **Example:** An e-commerce brand selling luxury skincare products could use AI to identify frequent online shoppers who have already purchased high-end beauty products.

3. **Hyper-Personalization:** Once you have your Dream 100, AI can help craft highly tailored messaging for each prospect. Tools like ChatGPT (yes, like me!) and Jasper AI can generate emails, ads, or proposals that speak directly to each prospect's unique needs and preferences.

    o **Example:** For a fitness equipment company targeting gyms, AI can create a personalized proposal for each gym in the Dream 100, highlighting how their equipment fits the gym's demographics and existing offerings.

The Human Element:

Even with AI, the human touch remains critical. AI can identify and analyze, but it's up to you to build the emotional connection. Combining the efficiency of AI with the empathy of a skilled salesperson creates a winning formula.

Education-Based Marketing: Teaching, Not Selling

One of Chet Holmes' most impactful concepts was **education-based marketing**, where businesses establish authority and trust by teaching their audience. In today's digital age, platforms like TikTok and YouTube provide the perfect stage for this strategy, allowing brands to educate millions in engaging, bite-sized formats.

Why Education-Based Marketing Works

1. **Builds Authority:** Teaching positions your brand as an expert. When you solve your audience's problems, they're more likely to trust you—and buy from you.
2. **Engages Emotionally:** People don't like being sold to, but they love learning. Education taps into curiosity and provides value, making your audience more receptive.
3. **Drives Long-Term Loyalty:** Educational content has a longer shelf life. A helpful video or infographic can continue to attract and nurture leads for months or even years.

Using TikTok and YouTube for Education-Based Marketing

These platforms are ideal for reaching Gen Z and Millennials, who prefer digestible, visual content.

1. **TikTok: Quick and Viral**
   o **Content Style:** Short, snappy, and visually engaging. Use trends, memes, and popular sounds to draw attention.
   o **Educational Example:** A financial services company could create a 15-second TikTok explaining "5 simple ways to save $500 this year."
   o **Call to Action:** End the video by directing viewers to your website or inviting them to follow for more tips.

Bonus Tip: Collaborate with influencers to boost credibility. Gen Z trusts recommendations from creators they admire.

2. **YouTube: Deep and Insightful**
   o **Content Style:** Longer-form, detailed, and value-packed. Think tutorials, how-tos, and explainer videos.
   o **Educational Example:** A tech company could upload a 10-minute video showing how their software solves common business challenges.
   o **Call to Action:** Include links in the video description for free trials, downloads, or consultations.

Key to Success: Storytelling

Both TikTok and YouTube thrive on storytelling. Frame your educational content as a journey:

- Start with a relatable problem.
- Explain how to solve it step-by-step.
- End with an inspirational takeaway or actionable advice.

Combining the Dream 100 and Education-Based Marketing

Imagine you've identified your Dream 100 prospects using AI. Here's how you can use education-based marketing to convert them into loyal customers:

1. **Research Each Prospect's Needs:** Use AI to learn what challenges they're facing. For instance, if a top prospect is a retail chain struggling with inventory management, tailor your content to address this issue.
2. **Create Customized Educational Content:** Develop videos, articles, or social media posts that solve the exact problems your

Dream 100 are facing. Share this content directly with your prospects.

o **Example:** A SaaS company could create a personalized YouTube playlist for each prospect, showcasing case studies and tutorials relevant to their industry.

3. **Engage Through Social Media:** Use TikTok to share snippets of your content in a fun, engaging way, and tag your Dream 100 prospects when appropriate. Follow up with direct outreach to encourage deeper conversations.

Case Study: Combining These Strategies

A luxury watchbrand wants to target its Dream 100 prospects—wealthy collectors and high-end retailers. Here's how they use AI and education-based marketing:

1. **AI Identifies the Dream 100:** The brand uses predictive analytics to find top prospects, such as boutique jewelry stores and influencers in the luxury space.
2. **TikTok for Awareness:** They create a TikTok series titled "Behind the Craft," showing the meticulous process of hand-assembling their watches.
3. **YouTube for Authority:** A YouTube mini-documentary dives deeper into the history of luxury timepieces, positioning the brand as an expert in craftsmanship.
4. **Personalized Outreach:** They send the Dream 100 exclusive links to their content, along with a personalized invitation to a virtual showcase.

The Bottom Line

The Dream 100 strategy and education-based marketing are timeless tools that have only become more powerful in the digital era. By combining AI's efficiency with the emotional connection of educational content, you can:

- Identify and reach your most valuable prospects.
- Build trust through teaching, not selling.
- Engage customers in the formats and platforms they love.

The result? A sales approach that feels human, resonates with today's digital-first audience, and drives lasting results.

SPIN Selling Meets SMART Sales – The Ultimate Framework for Modern Selling

Sales success is built on understanding and addressing customer needs. Neil Rackham's *SPIN Selling* introduced a game-changing approach to this by shifting the focus from aggressive selling to effective questioning. Let's revisit the core principles of SPIN Selling and then reimagine them as a modern, digital-friendly framework using **SMART**: a streamlined, action-oriented system for the limitless world of sales.

The SPIN Selling Principles: A Foundation of Effective Questioning

SPIN is an acronym that represents the four types of questions every salesperson should ask to understand and solve customer problems:

1. **S - Situation Questions:**
   o These questions gather information about the customer's current situation.
   o **Purpose:** Build context and rapport by understanding the customer's background, challenges, and goals.
   o **Example:** "How do you currently handle team collaboration in your organization?"

2. **P - Problem Questions:**
   o These questions uncover the pain points or challenges the customer faces.

o **Purpose:** Help the customer articulate their problems, setting the stage for your solution.

o **Example:** "What challenges do you face with your current system?"

3. **I - Implication Questions:**
   o These questions explore the consequences of the problems and make them feel urgent.
   o **Purpose:** Highlight the cost of inaction and the need for a solution.
   o **Example:** "What happens if you don't address these inefficiencies soon?"

4. **N - Need-Payoff Questions:**
   o These questions lead the customer to see the value of solving the problem and adopting your solution.
   o **Purpose:** Position your product or service as the ideal solution to their challenges.
   o **Example:** "How would it benefit your team if they could save 20% of their time each week?"

Evolving SPIN for the Modern World: Introducing SMART

SPIN Selling is highly effective, but the digital age demands a more dynamic, actionable framework that resonates with today's hyper-informed, digital-savvy customers. Enter **SMART**: a modern take on SPIN that focuses on guiding customers through the sales journey while embracing technology, personalization, and emotional intelligence.

SMART = Situation, Meaningful Problems, Amplify Implications, Reward-Oriented Needs, Tailored Solutions

S - Situation: Lay the Foundation

Before engaging with a customer, salespeople must deeply understand their context. In the digital era, this step is powered by technology.

How to Apply:

1. **Leverage AI and Data Analytics:**
   o Use tools like LinkedIn Sales Navigator, CRM platforms, or website tracking to gather insights about your prospects.
   o Example: "I noticed your company just launched a new product line. How has the reception been so far?"

2. **Social Media Listening:**
   o Study their social media activity to identify priorities, values, and challenges.
   o Example: "I saw your post about team productivity struggles. Is that something you're looking to improve?"

3. **Be Specific and Relatable:**
   o Avoid generic questions. Tailor your approach based on what you know.
   o Example: Instead of asking, "What's your company's focus right now?" say, "How is your team preparing for the upcoming product launch?"

M - Meaningful Problems: Discover What Truly Matters

Not all problems are created equal. To resonate with your customer, focus on uncovering the challenges that are most relevant and impactful to them.

How to Apply:

1. **Ask Questions That Go Beyond Surface-Level Issues:**

o Example: "What's the most frustrating aspect of your current software?"

2. **Identify Emotional Triggers:**
   o Example: "How does [problem] impact your team's morale?"

3. **Use Digital Tools to Spark Engagement:**
   o Example: Run polls or quizzes on LinkedIn or Instagram to ask prospects about their challenges. Use their responses to guide your follow-up questions.

A - Amplify Implications: Show the Ripple Effect

This is where the magic happens. Amplifying implications helps the customer realize the cost of ignoring their problems, creating urgency for a solution.

How to Apply:

1. **Highlight Real-World Consequences:**
   o Example: "If this issue continues, how will it impact your ability to meet end-of-year goals?"

2. **Use Data and Visuals:**
   o Share infographics, reports, or statistics that demonstrate the broader impact of their problem.
   o Example: "A recent study shows that companies lose an average of 30% productivity due to [problem]. Does that align with what you're seeing?"

3. **Incorporate Storytelling:**
   o Share relatable stories of other customers who faced similar issues and the consequences they experienced before resolving them.

o   Example: "One of our clients struggled with the same challenge, and it led to [specific negative outcome]. Here's how they turned it around."

R - Reward-Oriented Needs: Paint a Picture of Success

Focus on the benefits of solving the problem, especially in terms that align with your customer's goals and values.

How to Apply:

1. **Ask Visionary Questions:**
   o   Example: "How would it feel to eliminate that pain point and free up 10 hours a week for your team?"

2. **Leverage Social Proof:**
   o   Share testimonials or case studies that illustrate the rewards your solution brings.
   o   Example: "Here's how one of our clients increased efficiency by 40% using our platform."

3. **Tie Rewards to Emotions:**
   o   Example: "Imagine the peace of mind you'd have knowing this process is fully automated and error-free."

T - Tailored Solutions: Deliver the Perfect Fit

Customers expect personalized solutions, not one-size-fits-all pitches. Tailor your offering to their unique needs and values.

How to Apply:

1. **Personalize Recommendations:**
   o Use AI to create custom proposals based on the customer's data and preferences.
   o Example: "Based on what you've shared, here's how our solution could save your team $X and streamline operations."

2. **Use Interactive Demos:**
   o Example: Offer virtual walkthroughs or personalized trials that show exactly how your product fits their workflow.

3. **Focus on Collaboration:**
   o Involve the customer in designing the solution.
   o Example: "Which of these features do you think would benefit your team the most?"

How SMART Modernizes SPIN

SPIN	SMART	Key Difference
Focused on Questions	Focused on Actions	SMART integrates modern tools to drive actionable insights.
Linear Process	Dynamic and Adaptive	SMART adapts to the digital, omnichannel customer journey.
Transaction-Centric	Relationship and Value-Oriented	SMART emphasizes long-term value and emotional connection.

Case Study: SMART in Action

A SaaS company uses SMART to sell a collaboration tool:

1. **S (Situation):** AI identifies that a target company recently switched to hybrid work, creating new challenges.
2. **M (Meaningful Problems):** Sales rep discovers their current tool is clunky, leading to wasted time and frustration.
3. **A (Amplify Implications):** Rep highlights that inefficient tools could cost them $50,000 annually in lost productivity.
4. **R (Reward-Oriented Needs):** Demonstrates how the SaaS tool could cut collaboration time by 30% and boost team morale.
5. **T (Tailored Solutions):** Offers a free trial tailored to their team's specific workflow.

Conclusion: From SPIN to SMART—A Framework for the Digital Age

By evolving SPIN Selling into SMART, sales teams can embrace the power of modern technology and customer expectations. SMART not only teaches salespeople how to ask questions but also how to act on them—making it the perfect framework for today's limitless digital customers.

Redefining the Little Red Book: Timeless Lessons for Modern Sales

Why Jeffrey Gitomer's Lessons Matter More Today

Jeffrey Gitomer's *The Little Red Book of Selling* is more than a book; it's a manifesto for mastering the art of sales. Packed with actionable advice and memorable quotes, it distills decades of sales wisdom into timeless principles. Its central message is clear: sales is about value, relationships, and personal accountability.

But why do these lessons still matter in the digital-first world? Because while technology and customer behavior have evolved, the core principles of human connection and trust remain constant. Today, the challenge is to adapt these principles to new platforms, tools, and audiences—particularly the digital-savvy Gen Z and Millennials who demand authenticity, creativity, and meaningful engagement.

Core Lessons Reimagined for Today

1. People Don't Like to Be Sold—They Love to Buy

Gitomer's Principle: Customers hate being pushed but love to make decisions on their own terms. The key is to guide them, not pressure them.

Modern Approach:

- **Use Content to Educate, Not Sell:** Create value-packed content on TikTok, Instagram Reels, or YouTube that answers question or solves problems.
- **Foster Authenticity:** Share real stories, behind-the-scenes content, and unpolished moments to build trust.

"Empowering customers to buy is the new selling. It's not about persuasion; it's about collaboration."

2. Personal Branding Is Everything

Gitomer's Principle: Your personal brand is your sales superpower. Customers don't just buy products; they buy trust in you.

Modern Approach:

- **Be the Influencer:** Use social media to share insights and build trust with your audience.

- **Leverage Social Proof:** Highlight testimonials, case studies, and user-generated content to establish credibility.

Actionable Tip: Include a personal branding checklist for readers, such as:

- Define your unique value proposition.
- Post consistently on LinkedIn or TikTok to showcase your expertise.

3. Value First, Sales Second

Gitomer's Principle: Deliver value before asking for the sale. When you solve problems, you earn trust.

Modern Approach:

- **Free Tools and Resources:** Offer free trials, e-books, or calculators that solve common problems.
- **Gamify Value:** Create interactive experiences like quizzes or challenges that showcase your solution.

"In today's market, value is the gateway to trust, and trust is the foundation of sales."

4. Relationships Are Key

Gitomer's Principle: Genuine, long-term relationships lead to lasting success. Focus on people, not just transactions.

Modern Approach:

- **Build Communities:** Create exclusive Facebook Groups, Discord servers, or LinkedIn communities.

- **Engage on Social Media:** Reply to comments, share user stories, and celebrate customer milestones.

Interactive Feature: Add a checklist for relationship-building:

- Send thank-you notes after purchases.
- Follow up with personalized tips based on the customer's industry.

5. The Power of Self-Belief

Gitomer's Principle: A salesperson's mindset determines their success. Confidence, positivity, and resilience are non-negotiable.

Modern Approach:

- **Leverage Mindfulness:** Introduce techniques like journaling, affirmations, and meditation to cultivate a positive mindset.
- **Celebrate Small Wins:** Encourage readers to track daily achievements to stay motivated.

"In a world full of noise, creativity is your microphone."

Real-World Examples

1. People Don't Like to Be Sold—They Love to Buy

- **Case Study:** A SaaS company used TikTok to post relatable content about the frustrations of outdated software. They didn't push their product but provided educational, entertaining content that resonated with their audience. Result? A 40% increase in inbound leads.

2. **Value First, Sales Second**

- **Case Study:** A skincare brand created a free "Skin Type Quiz" that recommended personalized routines. Users received value before being sold products, leading to a 25% higher conversion rate.

3. **Relationships Are Key**

- **Case Study:** A fitness brand launched a private Discord community for customers to share progress and support each other. This fostered loyalty and boosted repeat purchases by 30%.

Interactive Exercise

Checklist: Building Your Personal Brand

1. What's your unique value proposition?
2. Which platforms will you use to engage your audience?
3. How will you showcase your expertise (e.g., articles, videos, or live Q&As)?

Relationship-Building Prompts

- Write a thank-you email or message to your last three customers.
- Send a personalized follow-up offering a resource or tip they'll find valuable.

Mindset Prompts

- Write down three things you're proud of from this week.
- Reflect on a challenge you overcame recently and how it helped you grow.

Jeffrey Gitomer's principles are timeless because they are rooted in understanding people—what they value, what they fear, and what they need. By embracing these lessons and adapting them for the limitless possibilities of the digital age, today's sales professionals can not only meet but exceed customer expectations.

"In today's market, value is the gateway to trust, and trust is the foundation of sales."

Gitomer's *Little Red Book of Selling* has shown us how to sell with heart, strategy, and purpose. Now, in the digital era, it's time to take these lessons to the next level—creating not just successful sales, but meaningful connections that last a lifetime.

Inbound Selling Reloaded: Connecting With Customers in the Modern World

Inspired by *Inbound Selling* by Brian Signorelli

Selling in a World That Comes to You

The days of interrupting customers with cold calls, generic emails, and flashy pitches are over. Today's customers don't want to be *sold to*—they want to discover solutions on their terms. Brian Signorelli's *Inbound Selling* highlights a powerful transformation in sales: the shift from outbound tactics to inbound strategies, where understanding, trust, and personalized value reign supreme.

For Gen Z and digital-first audiences, inbound selling isn't just a strategy—it's a way to connect with authenticity in a world where information and choices are limitless. Let's reimagine the principles of inbound selling to align with modern tools, platforms, and customer expectations.

Core Principles of Inbound Selling (Reimagined for Today)

1. **Meet Buyers Where They Are**

Signorelli's Insight: Buyers no longer rely on salespeople for information—they're already researching online. Sellers must adapt by meeting customers on the platforms they frequent and speaking their language.

Modern Approach:

- **Be Present on Digital Channels:** Today's buyers are on TikTok, Instagram, and LinkedIn. Use these platforms to provide value through relatable content.
- **Leverage Social Listening:** Tools like Hootsuite or Brandwatch can help you understand what prospects are talking about, their challenges, and where they're hanging out online.

If your audience spends hours scrolling TikTok, create engaging, informative videos that answer their questions or address their pain points in under 30 seconds.

2. **Personalize Every Interaction**

Signorelli's Insight: Inbound selling requires sellers to focus on the buyer's unique journey, tailoring every touchpoint to their needs and preferences.

Modern Approach:

- **Use AI for Personalization:** Tools like HubSpot or Salesforce can analyze customer data and help you craft highly targeted messages. For example, suggest solutions based on their browsing history or previous interactions.

- **Make It Feel Human:** Add a personal touch to emails, DMs, or video messages. Even a simple reference to something specific about the prospect (like their recent post or company achievement) can make all the difference.

Instead of sending a generic email, record a short, personalized video pitch using tools like Vidyard or Loom. Say, "Hi [Name], I saw your recent TikTok on [topic], and I think [product] could be a game-changer for your business."

3. **Align With the Buyer's Journey**

Signorelli's Insight: Inbound selling mirrors the buyer's journey: Awareness, Consideration, Decision. Salespeople must deliver value at each stage without being pushy.

Modern Approach:

- **Awareness:** Create educational content that solves problems before prospects even know they need a product.
- **Consideration:** Offer resources like webinars, live Q&As, or case studies to help prospects evaluate options.
- **Decision:** Provide personalized consultations or free trials to show how your solution fits seamlessly into their goals.

Example: A skincare brand creates a TikTok series:

1. Awareness: "5 signs your skincare routine might be damaging your skin."
2. Consideration: "Here's why dermatologists recommend [ingredient]."
3. Decision: "DM us for a free consultation and custom routine recommendation!"

4.　**Build Trust Through Value-Driven Content**

Signorelli's Insight: Buyers trust sellers who provide value before asking for anything in return. Inbound selling prioritizes teaching, not pitching.

Modern Approach:

- **Create Relatable Content:** Post educational and entertaining videos, infographics, or blogs that address your audience's needs.
- **Embrace Transparency:** Share pricing guides, product details, and even challenges your company has faced. Honesty builds credibility.

Example: A tech company posts Instagram Reels showing:

1. Behind-the-scenes clips of their team developing a new feature.
2. Tutorials for non-customers to solve common tech issues.
3. Testimonials from users who benefited from their product.

"Today's customers trust value over flash. If you teach them something useful, they'll come back for the solution."

5.　**Use Data Without Losing Humanity**

Signorelli's Insight: Inbound selling is data-driven but requires emotional intelligence to connect authentically with prospects.

Modern Approach:

- **Analyze Trends and Behaviors:** Use tools like Google Analytics, social media insights, or heatmaps to understand what your audience engages with most.
- **Inject Empathy:** While data provides insights, always lead with a human touch. Listen actively, ask thoughtful questions, and adapt to their emotions.

Example: A fitness app uses data to identify when users are most likely to drop off. They send personalized notifications like, "Hi [Name], we noticed you haven't logged a workout this week. Need a quick boost? Here's a 5-minute routine!"

Real-World Examples of Inbound Selling

1. Spotify: Meeting Buyers Where They Are

Spotify's "Discover Weekly" playlist anticipates user preferences based on their listening habits, delivering value before the user even realizes they want it. This aligns perfectly with the Awareness stage of the buyer's journey.

2. Glossier: Building Trust Through Value-Driven Content

Glossier became a cult favorite by creating relatable content that answered customers' skincare questions. Their Instagram is a blend of tutorials, reviews, and user-generated posts, making them approachable and trustworthy.

3. HubSpot: Aligning with the Buyer's Journey

As a pioneer of inbound selling, HubSpot offers free tools, webinars, and templates to attract prospects. Their strategy? Teach first, sell later.

Interactive Features for Readers

Inbound Selling Checklist

- **Are you meeting your buyers where they are?**
  - o Have you researched which platforms they use most?
  - o Do you have content tailored for each platform?

- **Are you personalizing your outreach?**
  - o Is your messaging relevant to the prospect's challenges or goals?
  - o Have you added a personal touch to your communication?

Prompts for Personalization

- What's one specific detail you know about your prospect that you can reference in your next email or call?
- How can you make your pitch feel more like a conversation and less like a script?

Buyer's Journey Map

- Awareness: What educational content can you create to attract prospects?
- Consideration: What resources can you offer to help them evaluate options?
- Decision: How can you make their buying experience seamless and personalized?

Inbound selling is more than a methodology, it's a mindset. It's about being where your customers are, speaking their language, and building trust by delivering value at every stage of their journey. For Gen Z, it's about authenticity, creativity, and personalization.

"Inbound selling isn't about chasing leads—it's about creating connections. The best sales happen when customers don't feel sold but supported."

By blending Signorelli's timeless principles with modern tools and strategies, today's sales professionals can thrive in a world where trust and personalization are the ultimate currencies.

The **digital Generation Z** is set to make up more than 90% of the salesforce in the future. Today, we can proudly call them the **Zales Team**—a team equipped with far more than just technological tools to craft a successful sales journey. Yet, the lessons of the past remain relevant and crucial in shaping the spirit of the Zales Team.

Among these timeless lessons are **The Power of Persistence** and **Turning Rejection into Resilience.** Here, we're reminded of the stories of **Thomas Edison** and **Colonel Sanders,** and others whose relentless determination turned obstacles into milestones of success.

The Power of Persistence

Edison didn't just invent the light bulb—he defined what it means to keep going. After thousands of attempts, he famously said, "I haven't failed. I've just found 10,000 ways that won't work." For Edison, each setback was just another step forward, a challenge to learn from.

His persistence went far beyond one invention. From the phonograph to the movie camera, Edison filed over 1,000 patents. His success wasn't some lucky break; it was fueled by relentless creativity, constant experimentation, and a refusal to give up. That's the power of persistence—turning each 'no' into just another part of the journey to 'yes.'

Turning Rejection into Resilience: The Colonel Sanders Story

Sales and rejection go hand in hand, but few people have turned rejection into opportunity like Colonel Harland Sanders, the creator of Kentucky Fried Chicken. Sanders faced more rejections than most would ever endure—rumor has it, he heard "no" over 1,000 times. But instead of giving up, he made every rejection a reason to keep going.

Sanders' journey was anything but smooth. Before he became "The Colonel," he ran a small diner that eventually burned down. Not one to quit, he rebuilt and decided to go big, taking his fried chicken recipe on the road. With his famous blend of herbs and spices in hand, he pitched his fried chicken to restaurant owners across the U.S., only to be met with closed doors and doubts about his recipe. But he didn't let the skepticism stop him.

Armed with a pressure cooker, Sanders drove across the country, cooking free samples for anyone willing to taste his chicken. He refined his recipe with each rejection, never wavering in his belief that he had something valuable to offer. Finally, after countless refusals, one restaurant owner agreed to partner with him on a revenue-sharing deal, launching the franchise that would grow into the KFC empire.

Sanders' story is a masterclass in resilience. He took every "no" as a step closer to success, using each rejection to fine-tune his recipe and pitch. His persistence didn't just make him a legend; it transformed fast food, creating a brand known worldwide.

The takeaway? Rejection doesn't define you or limit your success. If anything, it pushes you to innovate, improve, and prove your value. Sanders' story reminds us that resilience, self-belief, and relentless passion can turn even the hardest setbacks into a path to greatness. Every "no" is just fuel for your next "yes."

Lessons to Remember:

1. **Rejection is Part of the Process** – It's not a stop sign; it's a nudge to grow.
2. **Believe in Your Vision** – Your passion and confidence are what others eventually buy into.
3. **Keep Improving** – Use setbacks to refine, adapt, and elevate what you're offering.

Colonel Sanders didn't just sell fried chicken—he sold a lesson in persistence that reshaped an industry. His journey is a reminder that grit and belief in yourself can turn rejection into revolutionary success.

Just as persistence turned setbacks into success for Edison and Colonel Sanders, another sales legend took a different approach—one built on relationships and trust. Instead of simply pushing products, he mastered the art of connection, proving that loyalty and genuine care could turn customers into lifelong advocates. His name- Joe Girard, the world's greatest salesman.

The Legacy of Joe Girard: Sales Genius and Relationship Builder

Every sales team has that one standout, but Joe Girard was more than just a top performer—he was a legend. Recognized by the *Guinness Book of World Records* as the "world's greatest salesman," Girard didn't just set records; he set the standard. His journey proves that dedication, exceptional customer service, and genuine connections can redefine success in sales.

Joe started out as a car salesman in Detroit, but he was no ordinary salesman. He made it his mission to turn every customer interaction into a lasting relationship. He wasn't just selling cars; he was building trust and loyalty. To stay connected, Joe sent personalized birthday and anniversary cards to each of his clients—thousands of them! It was his way of saying, "You matter," and it worked. He stayed top-of-mind, and his clients kept coming back, often bringing friends and family along.

Joe's secret? He always went above and beyond for his clients. He wasn't about quick wins or fast deals; he was about creating an unforgettable experience. By delivering more than what was expected, Joe built a level of trust that set him apart from the competition. People trusted him not just because he sold good cars but because he genuinely cared.

It didn't happen overnight. Joe's success was a result of discipline, hard work, and a commitment to constant improvement. He tracked every client interaction, remembering details and tailoring his approach. This attention to detail and focus on improvement made him unstoppable.

At his peak, Joe was selling six cars a day, totaling over 1,400 a year—unheard-of numbers that earned him his world record. His story is a blueprint for anyone in sales, showing that true success isn't just about closing deals; it's about creating relationships that last.

Takeaways from Joe Girard's Story:

1. **Build Genuine Connections** – Going beyond transactions turns customers into loyal advocates.
2. **Exceed Expectations** – Surprise clients with exceptional service, and they'll keep coming back.
3. **Constantly Improve** – Attention to detail and refining your approach keeps you at the top of your game.

Joe Girard's story is a testament to the power of persistence, trust, and connection. His approach to sales isn't just a method—it's a mindset. By embracing his focus on relationships and a relentless drive to improve, every salesperson can aim not just to sell but to build a lasting legacy.

Here are several real stories of brilliant sales success, showcasing innovative strategies and powerful relationship-building techniques that transformed businesses:

- **FedEx's "Absolutely, Positively Overnight"**

  - **Background**: In the 1970s, FedEx was facing an uphill battle trying to sell its overnight delivery service. At the time, few businesses believed there was a need for such a service, and competitors doubted the company would last.

- **Sales Strategy**: FedEx founder Fred Smith introduced the slogan "When it absolutely, positively has to be there overnight," appealing to businesses in need of reliability. This slogan, combined with an aggressive sales campaign focused on reliability, established FedEx as a go-to for urgent deliveries.
- **Result**: FedEx's commitment to fulfilling its promise earned it widespread trust and loyalty, transforming it into a global leader in express transportation. Today, "overnight delivery" is almost synonymous with FedEx, proving the impact of targeted, need-driven messaging.

- ## IBM's Shift from Selling Products to Selling Solutions

  - **Background**: In the early 1990s, IBM was struggling as the personal computer industry became more competitive. Customers began shifting to smaller tech companies that could offer cost-effective solutions.
  - **Sales Strategy**: IBM made a strategic shift from selling products to selling solutions. Rather than focusing on hardware, they pivoted to becoming a provider of integrated IT solutions for businesses. Sales reps were trained to identify customer problems and propose customized solutions.
  - **Result**: IBM's solution-oriented approach rejuvenated the company and transformed it into a service-driven organization. Today, IBM's sales success is rooted in its deep customer relationships, built on solving specific challenges rather than pushing products.

- ## McDonalds and the Birth of the "Value Meal"

  - **Background**: In the 1980s, McDonald's noticed a trend where customers wanted a full meal but felt that it was expensive to buy items individually. The company needed to increase the average check size and enhance customer satisfaction.

- **Sales Strategy**: McDonald's developed the "Value Meal," a combo option that bundled a main item, fries, and a drink at a discounted price. This allowed customers to enjoy a complete meal at a reasonable price, making the purchasing decision easier.
- **Result**: The Value Meal concept drove higher sales volumes and significantly boosted McDonald's profits. This strategy was so successful that it became a staple in the fast-food industry, with other brands adopting similar offerings. It demonstrated the power of offering convenience and perceived value.

- **Apple's iPhone: Selling an Ecosystem**

  - **Background**: When Apple introduced the iPhone in 2007, the company not only entered a competitive market but also aimed to redefine the industry. Their strategy wasn't just to sell a phone but to create an ecosystem that customers would want to be a part of.
  - **Sales Strategy**: Apple positioned the iPhone not just as a standalone device but as part of a larger Apple ecosystem, integrated seamlessly with other products like the Mac, iPad, and Apple Watch. Sales associates emphasized this connectivity, and the unique experience Apple offered across devices.
  - **Result**: Apple's approach to selling an ecosystem rather than a product increased customer loyalty, boosted repeat purchases, and made switching to other brands less appealing. The strategy has since become a cornerstone of Apple's sales success and customer retention.

- **Netflix's Transition to Streaming and Personalized Recommendations**

  - **Background**: Originally a DVD rental service, Netflix faced a decline in demand as the industry shifted toward digital. They needed a transformative sales and marketing strategy to stay relevant.

- **Sales Strategy**: Netflix pivoted from DVD rentals to a subscription-based streaming service, making content instantly available. They also invested in developing a recommendation algorithm to personalize the viewing experience, increasing engagement and satisfaction.

- **Result**: Netflix's innovative approach made it a leader in streaming, ultimately transforming the entertainment industry. By personalizing recommendations, Netflix increased user engagement, minimized cancellations, and saw explosive growth. The strategy also positioned them as a pioneer in personalized content delivery.

- ## Toyota's Lean Sales Model with "Just-in-Time" Production

  - **Background**: In the 1950s, Toyota wanted to increase efficiency in manufacturing and meet consumer demands more effectively. However, they were limited in resources compared to American car manufacturers.

  - **Sales Strategy**: Toyota developed the "Just-in-Time" (JIT) production model, reducing waste by manufacturing only what was needed to meet demand. Sales teams provided real-time feedback on what customers wanted, allowing Toyota to respond to market needs with speed and precision.

  - **Result**: The JIT model enabled Toyota to reduce production costs and improve quality, leading to a stronger market position and increased sales globally. This efficiency and responsiveness became a key selling point for Toyota's cars, propelling it to become one of the world's largest automakers.

- **Zappos and the Customer-Centric Approach**

  - **Background**: Zappos, an online shoe retailer, entered a market where customers were hesitant to buy shoes online due to fit and comfort concerns.
  - **Sales Strategy**: Zappos made customer service their primary focus. They offered free returns, 24/7 customer service, and even sent replacement products at no cost if something went wrong. Their sales reps were trained to provide a "WOW" experience, prioritizing customer satisfaction over quick sales.
  - **Result**: Zappos's customer-centric approach built trust and loyalty, leading to high customer retention and repeat sales. It demonstrated that exceptional customer service could be a powerful differentiator in online retail, ultimately contributing to Zappos's acquisition by Amazon for nearly $1 billion.

Here are several notable sales success stories from Asia, showcasing how companies in this diverse region have creatively adapted to local market demands and transformed challenges into opportunities:

- **Alibaba's 11.11 Global Shopping Festival**

  - **Background**: When Alibaba launched its "Singles' Day" shopping event in 2009, it was a relatively unknown holiday. The concept was to celebrate being single by shopping online, and Alibaba's goal was to drive up sales during an otherwise quiet period.
  - **Sales Strategy**: Alibaba transformed Singles' Day into the world's largest shopping festival by creating an atmosphere of excitement with flash sales, huge discounts, and exclusive deals. They invested heavily in digital advertising and gamified the shopping experience, making it interactive and engaging. This event grew with the help of social media and collaboration with global brands.

- **Result**: Singles' Day became a global phenomenon, with Alibaba breaking sales records year after year. In 2020 alone, they generated over $74 billion (about $230 per person in the US) in sales. This innovative approach to e-commerce transformed an ordinary day into a massive retail event, inspiring similar shopping festivals worldwide.

- ## Xiaomi's Crowdsourced Product Development in China

  - **Background**: Xiaomi entered the smartphone market in China, where giants like Apple and Samsung dominated. Without the resources to compete head-on, Xiaomi had to find a different way to attract customers.
  - **Sales Strategy**: Xiaomi leveraged social media and engaged its community to develop products based on user feedback. They asked fans about features they wanted in a smartphone, allowing them to co-create and suggest changes, and launched their phones online with "flash sales." This approach built a community-driven brand where customers felt valued and invested in the product.
  - **Result**: Xiaomi's crowdsourced model helped it grow quickly and win over fans, who saw Xiaomi as "their" brand. Within just a few years, Xiaomi became one of the top smartphone brands in China and expanded globally, with this community-centric sales model as a cornerstone.

- ## Tata Nano: Creating the World's Cheapest Car in India

  - **Background**: In 2008, Tata Motors saw a gap in the Indian market for an affordable vehicle for the masses. Many families were still using motorcycles to transport multiple members, and a low-cost car could offer a safer, more comfortable alternative.

- **Sales Strategy**: Tata Motors launched the Tata Nano, positioning it as "the people's car" with a price tag of around $2,000, making it the world's cheapest car at the time. Their sales strategy focused on affordability and safety, targeting families who aspired to own a car but couldn't afford one.
- **Result**: Although the Nano faced production and perception challenges, Tata's efforts to make car ownership accessible to millions were groundbreaking. The Nano became a symbol of innovation in affordability, and Tata's broader strategy helped cement its reputation as a company dedicated to meeting the needs of India's population.

- **Samsung's "Next Big Thing" Campaign in South Korea**

  - **Background**: In the early 2000s, Samsung was primarily known as an electronics manufacturer but had yet to be recognized as a leading global smartphone brand. Competing with Apple, especially in Western markets, required a major shift in perception.
  - **Sales Strategy**: Samsung launched the "Next Big Thing" campaign, focusing on high-quality, cutting-edge technology, and establishing Samsung as an innovator. The campaign used humor and direct comparisons to Apple, positioning Samsung as a forward-thinking brand that offered unique features.
  - **Result**: The campaign was a major success, transforming Samsung into a household name in smartphones and technology. Samsung's smartphone sales skyrocketed, making it a top competitor in the global smartphone market, and their strong branding propelled them to global recognition.

- **Grab's Hyperlocal Approach to Ridesharing in Southeast Asia**

  - **Background**: Grab started as a small startup in Malaysia competing against Uber and other international giants. The challenge was that Southeast Asia's unique traffic, road, and regulatory conditions required a tailored solution.
  - **Sales Strategy**: Grab took a hyperlocal approach, adapting its services to each country's needs. They added features like cash payments, integrated local language support, and adapted to local regulations. Grab also expanded into other services, such as food delivery and digital payments, to become a "super app."
  - **Result**: Grab's localized approach allowed it to outmaneuver Uber and ultimately buy out Uber's operations in Southeast Asia. Today, Grab is a leading brand across the region, and its diversified services and community focus have helped it grow into a multi-billion-dollar company.

- **Uniqlo's "LifeWear" Philosophy in Japan**

  - **Background**: Uniqlo began as a small clothing store in Japan, but founder Tadashi Yanai had a vision to make it a global brand. With countless apparel competitors, Uniqlo needed a unique selling point to set it apart from fast fashion brands.
  - **Sales Strategy**: Uniqlo adopted a "LifeWear" philosophy, focusing on high-quality, functional clothing that was affordable and timeless, rather than trendy. They emphasized innovative materials and a minimalist design approach, targeting customers who valued quality and comfort over fast-changing fashion.
  - **Result**: This focus on functional, accessible fashion turned Uniqlo into one of the most successful clothing brands worldwide. Its success in Japan served as a launchpad, and today Uniqlo has become a beloved brand globally, emphasizing simplicity and quality over trends.

- ## OYO Rooms' Affordable Hospitality Revolution in India

  - **Background**: OYO Rooms began in India with the aim of standardizing the fragmented budget hotel industry. Many hotels had low standards and inconsistent services, creating a need for affordable yet reliable accommodation.
  - **Sales Strategy**: OYO created a network of partner hotels by standardizing rooms and amenities, providing a quality guarantee to guests. They also leveraged a strong online booking platform and offered attractive discounts to build a customer base. This strategy made it easier for travelers to find budget-friendly, reliable options.
  - **Result**: OYO's model was a massive success in India and quickly expanded to international markets. The brand became synonymous with affordable, quality accommodations, revolutionizing budget hospitality in Asia and beyond.

- ## The "Flexible Payment Plan" in Africa

  - **Location**: Kenya
  - **Story**: A sales rep for a solar energy company in Kenya was struggling to close deals with low-income households in rural areas. Although the product was in high demand, many potential customers simply couldn't afford the upfront cost of the solar units. Instead of giving up, the sales rep approached his manager with an idea: offer a flexible payment plan that allowed families to pay in small, manageable installments. The company adjusted its model, and with the new payment option, the rep saw an immediate increase in sales. Many households could now afford solar energy, creating positive word of mouth.
  - **Moral**: Flexibility and creativity in addressing financial barriers can make products more accessible, leading to both business success and customer loyalty.

- **The "Custom Solution" Success in Europe**

  - **Location**: Germany
  - **Story**: A tech sales manager was pitching a software solution to a German manufacturing company. Despite a great presentation, the client's team was hesitant because their specific needs weren't fully addressed by the standard product. Sensing the hesitancy, the sales manager proposed a tailored solution, offering to customize features to suit the client's operational requirements. After consulting with his development team, he created a prototype with the requested customizations and returned for a follow-up presentation. The client was impressed with the personalized approach and signed a long-term contract.
  - **Moral**: Listening to the client and being willing to adapt to their unique needs can turn a "no" into a "yes" and build lasting business relationships.

- **Turning Competition into Collaboration in Asia**

  - **Location**: Singapore
  - **Story**: In Singapore, a sales executive from a small logistics company was competing against a much larger competitor for a key account. Realizing that he couldn't match the larger company's pricing, he reached out to the competitor's sales team and proposed a collaborative bid. Together, they presented a joint solution that leveraged both companies' strengths, providing the client with faster and more cost-effective services. The client appreciated the innovative approach and awarded them the account.
  - **Moral**: Viewing competitors as potential collaborators can open up new business opportunities and create unique solutions for clients.

- ## The "Language Barrier" Lesson in Europe

  - **Location**: France
  - **Story**: A British sales rep was on a business trip in Paris, pitching a new line of high-end cosmetics to a French retailer. Although fluent in English, the French buyers struggled with some technical terms and cultural references, which made the presentation less engaging. Sensing this, the rep switched to basic French, apologized for not being fluent, and showed a genuine effort to communicate in their language. The clients appreciated the attempt and became more receptive to the pitch. The deal went through, and the relationship was stronger for it.
  - **Moral**: Making an effort to adapt to your client's language and culture shows respect and can bridge gaps, even if you're not perfectly fluent.

- ## Selling the Story, Not Just the Product in Africa

  - **Location**: South Africa
  - **Story**: A saleswoman for a sustainable fashion brand was promoting a new line of eco-friendly shoes in Cape Town. However, customers were hesitant because the products were priced higher than typical alternatives. Instead of pushing the product, she shared the brand's story, explaining how the shoes were made from recycled materials and ethically sourced resources, benefiting local communities. By focusing on the brand's mission, she connected emotionally with customers, who felt they were supporting a worthy cause. Sales soared, and the brand built a loyal following in the region.
  - **Moral**: Selling a product's story and purpose can create an emotional connection that transcends price concerns, building loyalty and driving sales.

- ## The "Long-Distance Trust" in Asia

  - **Location**: Japan
  - **Story**: An international sales director was working on a deal with a Japanese client. Despite weeks of virtual meetings and excellent negotiations, the Japanese client seemed hesitant to finalize the deal. Understanding the cultural importance of trust and personal connection in Japan, the director decided to travel there for an in-person meeting. He spent time not only discussing business but also getting to know the client over meals and small gatherings. This face-to-face effort reassured the client, who signed the deal by the end of the visit.
  - **Moral**: In some cultures, building trust requires a personal touch. Taking the time to meet in person can make a significant difference in closing deals, especially in relationship-driven markets.

- ## The "Small Gesture" that Closed a Big Deal in Europe

  - **Location**: Spain
  - **Story**: A sales rep was negotiating with a Spanish retailer for a long-term supply contract. Near the final stages, the retailer's representative mentioned that his young daughter's birthday was the following week. The rep noted this casually, but before the meeting ended, he arranged for a small, thoughtful gift to be delivered to the client's office for his daughter. This gesture wasn't extravagant, but it showed attention to detail and respect for personal relationships. The retailer was moved, and he signed the contract soon after.
  - **Moral**: Small, thoughtful gestures can strengthen client relationships and show that you care about them as individuals, not just as business partners.

- **Overcoming Resource Challenges in Africa**

  - **Location**: Nigeria
  - **Story**: A sales team was working on selling a new water purification system to local communities in Nigeria, but they struggled to find ways to convince people to invest in the system. One rep realized that showing the product in action could be more effective than verbal explanations. He arranged a demonstration at a community event, where people could see firsthand the benefits of clean water and taste it for themselves. The demonstration was a hit, leading to several immediate sales and a lot of positive word-of-mouth.
  - **Moral**: Sometimes, letting people experience the product firsthand is the best way to communicate its value, especially in resource-challenged markets.

- **Adapting to Unexpected Demands in Asia**

  - **Location**: South Korea
  - **Story**: A tech company was trying to sell software to South Korean educational institutions, but the initial feedback wasn't great. Schools found the software too complex for their needs. The company's sales lead decided to listen carefully to each institution's unique requirements and then relayed these to the product development team. The software was then modified to be more user-friendly and tailored to the educational system's specific needs. As a result, sales picked up quickly, and the product became widely adopted.
  - **Moral**: Flexibility and willingness to adapt a product to local needs can make the difference between a missed opportunity and widespread success.

CHAPTER 6

The Right Roles, Not Roulette: How AI Fixes Sales Teams

Meet Ryan, a young and ambitious sales manager at a fast-growing tech company. Ryan's team was full of talent, but they were struggling to meet their targets. Frustrated, Ryan decided to shake things up. He reassigned roles without much thought—hoping that a little "change" would spark results.

He put Sarah, the empathetic relationship builder, in charge of cold calls. Meanwhile, he gave Jamal, the number-crunching analytics genius, the task of managing client relationships. The logic? Sarah needed to "toughen up," and Jamal needed to get "out of his shell."

The result? A disaster.

Sarah, who excelled at nurturing long-term clients, froze under the pressure of constant rejection on cold calls. Jamal, who thrived behind the scenes analyzing data, struggled to connect with clients on a personal level. Deals started falling through, morale dropped, and the company's growth stalled.

Ryan had sent his "horse" to plow the field and his "donkey" to race— and just like the saying, they lost both the harvest and the bet.

The Lesson

In the world of sales, everyone has strengths, and success depends on playing to those strengths. Forcing people into roles that don't match their talents is like sending the wrong team to do the wrong job, it wastes potential, damages results, and lowers morale.

In Ryan's case, the fix was simple. He took a step back, reassessed his team, and realigned roles based on strengths. Sarah went back to managing key accounts, where her empathy shined. Jamal returned to analyzing data and identifying high-potential leads for the team to target. Within months, the team not only recovered but exceeded their goals.

Know your strengths and those of your team. The key to winning in sales—or any field—is putting the right people in the right roles. Everyone doesn't have to do everything; they just need to do what they're best at.

Sales is like a well-orchestrated symphony—when everyone plays their part, the results are harmony and success.

Beyond the Buzz: AI's Real Impact on Sales

Imagine this: you're a salesperson 10 years ago, juggling spreadsheets, cold calls, and endless guesswork just to connect with leads. Fast forward to today, and AI is your secret weapon—automating tasks, analyzing data, and personalizing every interaction. It's not just about making sales faster; it's about making them smarter, more precise, and deeply meaningful.

Here's how AI has redefined the sales game, one step at a time.

- **Lead Scoring and Prioritization: From Guesswork to Precision**

The Struggle Back Then:

Sales reps would sift through piles of spreadsheets or CRM data, relying on their instincts to decide which leads were worth chasing. Often, this meant wasting time on unqualified leads or missing out on golden opportunities.

The AI Difference Today:

AI tools like Salesforce Einstein or HubSpot analyze lead behavior, demographics, and engagement history in seconds. They score leads based on their likelihood to convert, flagging the hottest prospects for immediate follow-up.

Storytime Example:

A SaaS sales team used to spend hours sorting through trade show sign-ups, unsure who to prioritize. Now, AI ranks lead based on actions like email opens and webinar attendance. Instead of guessing, reps know exactly where to focus, cutting lead qualification time by half and doubling conversion rates.

- **Sales Forecasting: From Uncertainty to Confidence**

The Struggle Back Then:

Forecasting sales used to mean staring at last year's numbers and crossing your fingers. Spreadsheets couldn't account for real-time factors like market shifts or emerging trends, making predictions unreliable.

The AI Difference Today:

AI tools like Gong or Clari take forecasting to another level. They analyze live sales data, economic trends, and deal progress to provide accurate, up-to-date projections. AI even spots patterns and anomalies, helping teams predict which deals are likely to close and when.

Storytime Example:

A retail chain once guessed holiday sales based solely on last year's numbers. Today, AI integrates local weather forecasts, online search trends, and social media buzz. The result? Inventory and marketing plans that perfectly match demand, reducing overstock and boosting revenue.

- **Personalized Outreach: From Generic to Hyper-Customized**

The Struggle Back Then:

Sales reps relied on generic email templates and cold calls, often hoping that a basic "Hi [First Name]" would grab attention. Personalization barely scratched the surface.

The AI Difference Today:

AI tools like Outreach.io craft hyper-personalized emails by analyzing customer behavior and preferences. AI chatbots start conversations at scale, qualifying leads and answering questions instantly.

Storytime Example:

A financial advisor used to blast emails offering generic services. Today, AI suggests personalized investment plans based on a prospect's LinkedIn activity and search history. The result? Response rates skyrocket, and conversations feel genuinely tailored.

- ### Real-Time Sales Assistance: From Memory to Instant Insights

The Struggle Back Then:

During sales calls, reps relied solely on their training and memory to answer questions. Important customer cues often went unnoticed, and valuable opportunities slipped through the cracks.

The AI Difference Today:

AI tools like Gong or Chorus.ai provide real-time prompts during calls, suggesting responses based on the conversation. They analyze tone, keywords, and sentiment to help reps steer discussions effectively.

Storytime Example:

A software sales rep once struggled to address objections during calls. Now, AI detects hesitation in a customer's tone and suggests sharing a relevant case study or offering a discount on the spot. The result? Objections turn into opportunities and deals close faster.

- ### Cross-Selling and Upselling: From Gut Instinct to Data-Driven Recommendations

The Struggle Back Then:

Cross-selling and upselling relied on reps' instincts or manual data review, which often missed key opportunities to add value for customers.

The AI Difference Today:

AI analyzes purchase history, usage patterns, and behavior to recommend complementary products or services automatically. Tools like Amazon's AI make it seamless.

Storytime Example:

A gym consultant once manually tracked members who might benefit from personal training. Now, AI monitors gym check-ins and app usage, identifying members ready for upgrades. Automated recommendations lead to a 30% boost in upsell revenue.

AI Enhances Both Speed and Quality

AI doesn't just make sales faster; it makes them smarter. By automating repetitive tasks, delivering real-time insights, and enabling deeper personalization, AI ensures every interaction is meaningful.

The Future of Sales with AI: What's Next?

Imagine a world where AI does even more. The future isn't about replacing salespeople—it's about empowering them to do their best work. Here's a glimpse of what's ahead:

- **Virtual Sales Assistants**

AI-powered virtual assistants will handle the heavy lifting, qualifying leads, scheduling meetings, and conducting discovery calls.

Future Scenario:

A B2B AI assistant interacts with a potential client via video. It asks qualifying questions, notes specific challenges, and passes the lead to a human rep fully briefed and ready to close.

- **Immersive Sales Experiences**

AR and VR, powered by AI, will make shopping immersive and interactive.

Future Scenario:

A furniture store lets customers use AR to see how a couch fits in their living room, complete with color-matching suggestions from AI.

- **Predictive Buyer Behavior**

AI will anticipate customer needs before they even realize them.

Future Scenario:

An e-commerce platform notices a customer browsing wedding-related content and proactively offers bridal packages, from gift registries to honeymoon deals.

- **Hyper-Personalized Sales Journeys**

Every customer journey will be uniquely designed by AI, adapting in real-time to their behavior.

Future Scenario:

A car dealership tracks buyer's website clicks, showroom visits, and social media activity. AI tailors the sales experience, from offering virtual test drives to sending exclusive discounts.

- **Emotional AI for Empathetic Interactions**

AI will read facial expressions, tone, and body language to respond empathetically.

Future Scenario:

In a healthcare setting, an AI-powered chatbot detects anxiety in a customer's tone while discussing insurance options. It adjusts its approach, schedules a follow-up, and reassures the customer with additional resources.

The Future Is Fast, Smart, and Personal

AI isn't just a tool—it's a game-changer. It blends speed with precision, making sales processes not just efficient but delightful for the customer. Whether it's crafting hyper-personalized emails or predicting future needs, AI ensures that every interaction feels intuitive and human.

"The future of sales isn't about selling harder—it's about connecting smarter. With AI, every interaction becomes a chance to understand, engage, and delight."

AI isn't just streamlining sales—it's leveling up the entire game. The future of selling isn't about reacting; it's about predicting what customers want before they even know it. With AI shaping buyer behavior, personalizing every move, and even reading emotions, the sales experience is about to get smarter, smoother, and more human than ever. Here's how.

Closing the Sales Loop: A Smart Seller's Strategy

Imagine this: You're a sales professional, and instead of just solving a single problem for your customer, you identify a way to tackle multiple pain points in one go. Not only do you meet their expectations, but you also create a win-win situation where you exceed your sales goals and deliver exceptional value to the client. This is the art of **closing the sales loop**—*a skill that turns a good salesperson into a sales visionary.*

Let me tell you a real story of how one smart sales manager turned a logistical nightmare into a seamless solution that not only secured a deal but redefined how a business operated.

The Challenge: A Logistical Maze

A Gulf-based oil company operating in remote fields of Kazakhstan had over 2,000 employees, mostly from the Middle East. Every week, more than 150 employees traveled back to the Middle East and North Africa. Add to that the regular shipments of supplies and spare parts from Dubai to Kazakhstan, and you had a logistical nightmare.

Flights were inconvenient and exhausting. Employees traveled long distances overland to reach the capital's airport, where they faced multi-leg journeys across several countries to get home. On top of that, the company spent heavily on shipping and supplies, coordinating multiple vendors and timelines. It was inefficient, costly, and frustrating for everyone involved.

The Visionary Sales Manager Steps In

*Enter the **smart sales manager** from a regional travel agency that handled the company's employee travel arrangements. He didn't just see the situation as a series of individual transactions; he saw the big picture.*

*By analyzing the company's travel, shipping, and supply needs, he realized that a single, comprehensive solution could solve multiple problems simultaneously. His idea? A **charter flight service** designed specifically for the company's unique needs.*

The Solution: A Charter Flight Loop

The sales manager proposed a weekly charter flight that would:

1. **Start near the company's remote site in Kazakhstan**, *eliminating the long overland journeys to the airport.*

2. ***First stop in Jordan***, *where employees could easily connect to destinations in North Africa.*
3. ***Continue to Beirut***, *offering more connectivity to other regions.*
4. ***Finish in Dubai***, *where the aircraft would load supplies, spare parts, and other goods before returning to Kazakhstan.*

This "sales loop" addressed every pain point:

- ***For the employees***: *It dramatically reduced travel time and fatigue.*
- ***For the company***: *It consolidated travel and shipping operations, cutting costs significantly while improving efficiency.*
- ***For the travel agency***: *It secured not only the company's ticketing business but also their shipping and logistics needs, creating a massive boost in revenue.*

The Results: A Win-Win Solution

The charter flight loop became a game-changer:

- *The company saved money by merging travel and shipping logistics into one streamlined operation.*
- *Employees were happier and more productive, thanks to shorter, more comfortable travel routes.*
- *The travel agency gained a significant boost in revenue, expanding its services beyond ticketing to manage the company's entire logistical operation.*

This wasn't just a deal—it was a partnership built on innovative thinking and value creation.

Key Takeaways for Closing the Sales Loop

Think Beyond Transactions: *Don't just sell a product or service; look for ways to solve multiple problems with a single solution.*

o   *For example: Instead of selling software licenses individually, offer a bundle that includes training, integration support, and long-term updates.*

Understand the Bigger Picture: *Take the time to deeply analyze your client's operations, pain points, and inefficiencies. The best ideas often come from understanding what they don't even realize they need.*

o   *For example: A hardware supplier notices their client's struggle with inventory tracking and offers a supply chain management system alongside their products.*

Create Win-Win Opportunities: *The best sales loops benefit everyone involved. If your solution saves the client money or time while boosting your revenue, you've struck gold.*

o   *For example: A subscription-based service offers discounted yearly plans that save the client money while locking in long-term business.*

The Role of AI in Closing the Sales Loop

In today's digital age, AI can supercharge your ability to close the sales loop. Here's how:

- **Data Analysis**: *AI can analyze customer behavior, operational inefficiencies, and spending patterns to identify opportunities for bundling or streamlining services.*
  - o   *Example: A logistics company uses AI to analyze a client's shipping routes, discovering inefficiencies. They propose consolidated routes that cut costs and delivery times, winning the client's loyalty.*
- **Predictive Insights**: *AI can forecast future needs based on historical data, helping sales teams propose proactive solutions.*

    o   *Example: An AI system at a retail supplier identifies seasonal spikes in demand and suggests stocking strategies, boosting both the supplier's and client's revenue.*

- ***Personalization at Scale***: *AI enables sales teams to craft tailored solutions for even the most complex clients.*
  - o   *Example: A telecom provider uses AI to analyze a client's data usage, offering a customized plan that bundles mobile, internet, and cloud services into one cost-effective package.*

Why This Matters

Gen Z loves efficiency, innovation, and solutions that make life easier. They value brands and salespeople who see the bigger picture and offer more than just a product—they want ecosystems that work seamlessly. For this generation, closing the sales loop isn't just smart; it's essential.

Example:

A streaming service notices a Gen Z user who frequently downloads workout videos. Instead of just suggesting more fitness content, the service partners with a fitness app to offer a bundle: exclusive workout videos plus a free trial of premium app features. This tailored approach feels effortless to the user and boosts the value for both companies.

Final Thought: Closing the Sales Loop Is About Creating Value

Closing the sales loop is a mindset, not just a strategy. It's about seeing beyond the immediate transaction and creating solutions that deliver value for everyone involved. Whether it's consolidating operations, offering tailored bundles, or leveraging AI to spot hidden opportunities, the art of the sales loop is what separates good salespeople from great ones.

"Smart sales don't just close deals, they close gaps, solve problems, and build systems that keep customers coming back for more."

The SALES Revolution: From Persuasion (Features) to Personalization (Futures)

Imagine stepping into the sales world of the past, where deals were closed by sheer charisma, charm, and persistence. The salesperson was the master of persuasion, weaving words to win over customers. This world, while impressive in its own way, was rooted in intuition and tradition. Now, fast-forward to today, where sales is less about a single charismatic closer and more about a collaborative, data-driven, and customer-centric experience. Let's explore this journey from functionals comparison angle of S.A.L.E.S which clearly shows that Sales is no longer static it is dynamic, adaptable and constantly evolving:

SALES in the Past: The Traditional Hustle

S - Selling Skills

Back then, the heart of sales was the "gift of the gab." A great salesperson didn't just sell a product—they sold themselves. Persuasion and personal charisma were the golden tools, turning even skeptics into buyers.

A - Advertising

Marketing was loud and broad—radio jingles, flashy TV ads, and bold print campaigns ruled the day. It didn't matter if it hit anyone or just a few. The idea was simple: cast the widest net and hope the right fish bit.

L - Leads

Leads were numbers in a Rolodex, names on a list, or random cold calls to strangers. Quantity often trumped quality, as the belief was that more calls meant more chances to close a deal.

E - Experience (Product-Centric)

The spotlight was on the product, not the person buying it. Salespeople memorized features and rattled off benefits, but rarely asked, "How can this make your life better?"

S - Success Metrics

It was all about the bottom line: How many products sold? How much revenue generated? Success was defined in spreadsheets and quotas, with little thought for the long-term relationships being built—or broken.

SALES Today: A New Digital Chapter

Now, let's step into the sales arena of today—a world built for digital natives and guided by innovation. It's not about selling; it's about solving. It's not about pushing; it's about personalizing.

S - Sustainability

Today's customers don't just want a great product; they want to feel good about buying it. Ethical practices, eco-conscious packaging, and a company's social impact matter as much as the product itself. Sustainability isn't an afterthought—it's the foundation of trust with modern consumers.

A - AI and Automation

The once-human-only intuition is now turbocharged by technology. AI predicts what customers want before they know it themselves. Chatbots answer questions at lightning speed. Automation personalizes every interaction, making customers feel valued and understood.

L - Leveraging Data

Gone are the days of guessing what a customer might like. Real-time data and advanced analytics provide a clear map of what drives customer behavior. It's not about fishing in the dark; it's about targeting with precision.

E - Engaging Experiences

Sales is no longer a transaction; it's an experience. Whether it's an interactive online store, personalized product recommendations, or virtual try-ons, today's sales journeys are designed to delight and engage customers at every touchpoint.

S - Scalable Solutions

Businesses today don't just think big—they think smart. Systems are designed to grow without breaking a sweat, from global e-commerce platforms to seamless omnichannel strategies that connect with customers wherever they are.

Past vs. Present: A World Transformed

Aspect	Past SALES	Modern SALES
Approach	Product-Centric	Customer-Centric
Technology	Minimal	Integral (AI, automation)
Sales Process	Manual and Intuitive	Data-Driven and Automated
Customer Focus	Generalized	Personalized and Targeted
Sustainability	Rarely Considered	Core Element
Metrics	Volume-Based	Experience and Loyalty-Based
Channels	Physical and Broad	Digital and Omnichannel

Key Takeaway:

In the modern **SALES** strategy, the customer experience is the **cornerstone**. It's no longer about just selling a product—it's about delivering **value, trust, and memorable interactions** that drive loyalty and long-term success.

Understanding how sales has evolved—from the traditional hustle to today's data-driven, customer-centric approach—is crucial. But no matter how much the landscape changes, one thing remains constant: **the power of a great pitch.** Whether you're selling a product, an idea, or yourself, the ability to capture attention in a short amount of time is a skill that transcends trends. And in today's fast-moving, short-form world, there's no better example of this than the **elevator pitch.**

Mastering the Art of Pitching: The Elevator Pitch Revolution

Picture this: You step into an elevator, and next to you is the CEO of a company you've been dying to partner with. The clock starts ticking. By the time the elevator doors open, you have one chance—just 60 seconds—to grab their attention, share your idea, and leave a lasting impression.

This is the magic of an **elevator pitch**. It's not just about talking fast—it's about delivering the essence of your idea with clarity, confidence, and impact. Gen Z, with its fast-paced, digital-native mindset, thrives on this kind of concise, punchy communication. But how do you nail it every time? Meet the **INVEST Pitching Framework**, a modern guide to crafting pitches that stick.

INVEST: The Formula for a Killer Pitch

INVEST isn't just a word, it's a philosophy. Each letter represents a key component that transforms a good pitch into a great one. Here's how it works:

I - Insight

Your pitch must start with a bang, and that means offering a fresh perspective or revealing an untapped opportunity. People listen when they learn something new.

Storytime Example:

Imagine pitching a sustainable fashion app. You start with, *"Did you know 85% of textiles end up in landfills? What if your next outfit could help change that?"* Insight hooks people, it makes them curious to hear more.

N - Need

Identify the pain point or problem your idea solves. A great pitch addresses a specific need, making it immediately relevant to your audience.

Storytime Example:

When pitching a coworking space to freelancers, you might say, *"Many freelancers feel isolated, struggling to balance productivity and community. Our coworking hub isn't just a space—it's where work meets belonging."* Highlight the need, and you've got their attention.

V - Value

Explain the tangible value your idea brings. How will it save time, money, or resources? What benefits does it deliver?

Storytime Example:

For a meal-prep subscription service, you could say, *"Our plans save the average household 5 hours a week and cut food waste by 30%. That's time back in your life and money back in your pocket."* Value shows them the payoff of saying "yes."

E - Experience

Paint a picture of the experience your product or service creates. How will it make your audience feel? What's the journey you're offering?

Storytime Example:

For a wellness app, you might pitch, *"Imagine waking up stress-free because your day is already planned for you. Our app turns your daily chaos into calm."* Experience helps people see themselves using your product.

S - Superiority

This is where you shine. What makes you better than the competition? Why should they choose you over anyone else?

Storytime Example:

For a tech startup, you could say, *"Unlike others, our platform uses AI to predict market trends, giving you an edge before your competitors even see what's coming."* Superiority shows why you're the best choice.

T - Transformation

End your pitch with the bigger picture—the change your idea will create. Transformation is the emotional clincher that makes your pitch unforgettable.

Storytime Example:

For a green energy solution, you might conclude, *"With your support, we won't just power homes—we'll power a cleaner future for generations to come."* Transformation ties your idea to a greater mission.

Why Gen Z Loves INVEST

Gen Z is all about authenticity, impact, and speed. They don't want fluff or filler—they want pitches that are bold, concise, and meaningful. The INVEST framework fits perfectly into their world:

- **Insight:** Appeals to their curiosity.
- **Need:** Aligns with their problem-solving mindset.
- **Value:** Speaks to their pragmatism.
- **Experience:** Creates emotional connection.
- **Superiority:** Satisfies their demand for the best.
- **Transformation:** Resonates with their desire to make a difference.

The Role of Technology in Pitching

In the digital era, your pitch doesn't stop at words. Technology amplifies your message, making it more engaging and impactful. Here's how:

- **AI Tools:** Platforms like ChatGPT can help refine your pitch, ensuring it's clear and compelling.
- **Presentation Apps:** Tools like Canva or Prezi make visuals pop, bringing your pitch to life.
- **Analytics:** Tools like LinkedIn Insights can help you tailor your pitch to your audience's interests.

Storytime Example:

A startup founder uses AI to analyze market trends, ensuring their pitch aligns with investors' priorities. During the presentation, interactive visuals highlight key data points, leaving a lasting impression. Technology doesn't just support the pitch—it elevates it.

Mastering the sales loop isn't just about closing deals—it's about how you close them. The approach you take can define whether your sales strategy builds trust and long-term success or burns bridges and damages reputations. In today's fast-paced, hyper-connected world, every sales interaction falls into one of three categories: ethical and value-driven, short-sighted and transactional, or downright deceptive. Let's break down The Good, The Bad, and The Ugly of Sales and explore what separates winning strategies from those that lead to failure.

The Good, The Bad, and The Ugly of Sales: A Modern Hypothesis

Sales is a lot like a classic Western movie—full of drama, triumph, and lessons about human nature. Drawing inspiration from Clint Eastwood's legendary *The Good, the Bad, and the Ugly*, let's dive into the wild world of modern sales. In today's digital-first era, every sales interaction can be categorized into these three archetypes: the **Good Sale**, the **Bad Sale**, and the **Ugly Sale**.

Think of this as your modern roadmap through the dusty trails of the sales frontier—learning what to aim for, what to avoid, and what to never let happen again.

The Good Sale: Where Sales Meets Integrity

The **Good Sale** is what every salesperson should aspire to. It's about creating value for the customer, solving their problems, and building long-term trust. In this scenario, the customer walks away feeling empowered, and the salesperson achieves their goals without resorting to tricks or pressure tactics.

Characteristics of a Good Sale:

1. **Transparency**: The buyer knows exactly what they're getting.
2. **Empathy**: The salesperson listens and tailors the solution to the buyer's needs.
3. **Long-term Thinking**: The focus is on building a relationship, not just closing a deal.

Example:

A subscription-based fitness app noticed that some users were struggling with advanced workouts. Instead of pushing upsells, they introduced a "Beginner's Plan" tailored to those who wanted to start slow. The move not only improved retention but also built loyalty among customers who felt understood and valued.

The Bad Sale: Short-Term Gains, Long-Term Pain

The **Bad Sale** is one where the salesperson may achieve their immediate target but at the expense of the customer's trust or satisfaction. It's often driven by desperation, pressure, or a lack of understanding of the customer's needs. These sales might win the battle but lose the war.

Characteristics of a Bad Sale:

1. **Overpromising**: Making commitments the product or service can't keep.
2. **Misalignment**: Selling something that doesn't fit the customer's actual needs.
3. **Short-Sightedness**: Prioritizing the close over the relationship.

Example:

A car dealership sells an SUV to a city-dweller who only needs a compact car. The salesperson convinced the buyer by touting unnecessary features like off-road capabilities. A month later, the customer is unhappy with the high fuel costs and cumbersome parking, leaving a scathing review online. That one sale cost the dealership future referrals and a tarnished reputation.

The Ugly Sale: Ethics on the Line

The **Ugly Sale** is where things get dark. This type of sale relies on manipulation, deceit, or outright exploitation. It's the scam of the sales world, leaving customers feeling duped and often causing irreparable damage to the brand.

Characteristics of an Ugly Sale:

1. **Deception**: Deliberately misleading the buyer.
2. **Exploitation**: Taking advantage of the buyer's lack of knowledge or urgency.
3. **Damage**: Leaving the customer worse off than before.

Example:

A shady online store promotes a "luxury smartwatch" at a steep discount, only to ship a cheap knockoff that barely works. While the company pockets quick cash, the flood of refund requests, bad reviews, and chargebacks forces it to shut down within months. This is the epitome of the Ugly Sale—profiting at the cost of ethics and longevity.

The Good Sale Teaches Us: Value Wins

Customers don't just buy products; they buy experiences, trust, and solutions. If you aim to deliver real value, your sales will not only grow but also sustain themselves through loyalty and referrals.

The Bad Sale Warns Us: Think Beyond Today

Shortcuts might seem tempting, but they'll come back to haunt you. Every customer interaction is an opportunity to build trust, and failing to do so will cost more than you gain.

The Ugly Sale Reminds Us: Ethics Matter

In a world of online reviews, social media, and viral stories, reputation is everything. The Ugly Sale might bring quick wins, but it guarantees long-term losses.

Modern-Day Sales Examples: The Good, the Bad, and the Ugly

The Good Sale: Patagonia's Commitment to Sustainability

Patagonia doesn't just sell outdoor gear—it sells a mission. By encouraging customers to repair old gear instead of buying new,

Patagonia demonstrates its value, building a loyal customer base that aligns with its brand ethos.

The Bad Sale: Streaming Subscription Pushes

A streaming service offers a free trial but buries the subscription details in fine print, leading to unexpected charges. Customers cancel en masse, leaving negative reviews about the lack of transparency.

The Ugly Sale: Fake Influencers

A "luxury" skincare brand pays fake influencers to promote its products with staged before-and-after photos. Once customers realize the scam, the brand faces lawsuits, refunds, and irreparable damage.

AI's Role in Keeping Sales Good

In the modern sales landscape, AI can act as a guide to keep your sales practices aligned with **Good Sales** principles:

- **AI for Personalization**: Platforms like Salesforce Einstein analyze customer data to offer tailored solutions, ensuring relevance and avoiding mismatched pitches.
- **AI for Transparency**: Chatbots can provide clear, consistent answers to customer questions, reducing the chance of overpromising.
- **AI for Feedback**: Sentiment analysis tools help monitor customer satisfaction, flagging issues before they escalate into Bad or Ugly Sales territory.

Storytime Example:

An AI-driven CRM at an e-commerce company tracks customers who abandon carts due to high shipping fees. Instead of aggressively pushing discounts, the system suggests alternatives like bundling purchases to save on costs. The approach feels collaborative, boosting conversions while maintaining trust.

How Gen Z Fits Into the Picture

Gen Z doesn't just buy products—they buy into brands. They value authenticity, transparency, and ethics, making them particularly sensitive to the type of sales approach a business uses. To win over Gen Z:

- **Be Honest**: Overpromising or manipulating won't work—they'll call you out on social media.
- **Add Value**: Show them why your product matters and how it aligns with their values.
- **Build Relationships**: Gen Z prefers brands they can trust over time, not quick pitches.

The Final Word: Be the Hero of Your Own Sales Story

In the sales frontier, you get to decide which character you'll play: the Good, the Bad, or the Ugly. Choose to deliver value, build trust, and align with your customer's needs. In a world full of noise, the Good Sale always stands out—and the Good Salesperson always wins.

"Sales isn't just about closing deals—it's about choosing the role you want to play in your customer's story. Be the hero, not the villain."

CHAPTER 7

Beyond the Horizon

Spotting Sales Blind Spots and Navigating Black Spots in the Digital Era

Imagine this: You're on a road trip with your best friends, music blasting, and the world zooming by. Everything is perfect—until you almost sideswipe a car hidden in your blind spot. It wasn't on your radar, but it was there, waiting to cause chaos. Now, think about sales. Every pitch, every call, every deal has its own "blind spots" and "black spots"—hidden pitfalls that can derail success in ways you don't see coming.

For Gen Z sales professionals who grew up with digital-first mindsets, navigating these shadows is both a challenge and an opportunity. Let's dive into these unseen obstacles, why they exist, and how you can flip the script to not just avoid them, but use them to your advantage.

Blind Spots vs. Black Spots: The Difference

- Blind Spots: The things you *don't know you're missing*. Think of them as the uncharted territories in your sales process. They're sneaky and dangerous because you don't even know they're there.

- Black Spots: The *known but hidden* dangers—places where mistakes and missteps tend to lurk. They're like that foggy patch on a road where you know how to slow down, but sometimes forget.

Both can trip you up, but they also offer a chance to grow if you learn to spot them early.

The Struggle

Let's talk about Mike, a rising star at a tech startup. Mike had everything: charm, tech-savviness, and killer closing skills. But he had one big blind spot—he didn't understand his customers' deeper pain points. During a pitch to a big client, he delivered a slick presentation packed with features, but the client's CEO interrupted: "This is great, but how does it solve our problem?" Mike froze.

The deal didn't close. Why? Mike missed the blind spot: *he was so focused on selling, he forgot to listen.*

Why Do Blind and Black Spots Exist?

1. Overconfidence in Your Pitch
   When you think you know everything, you stop asking questions. Confidence is great, but overconfidence blinds you to red flags.

2. The Digital Fog
   AI and automation are incredible, but they can create distance. Relying too much on tools can make you lose the human touch.

3. Customer Mistrust
   Gen Z buyers, like Gen Z sellers, value authenticity. If you come off as too "salesy" or inauthentic, they'll disengage fast.

4. Data Overload
   With so much information at your fingertips, it's easy to drown in data and miss the signals that really matter.

Modern Insights for Navigating Blind Spots

- **Listening Like a Detective**

Every prospect leaves breadcrumbs—hints about their real needs, fears, and goals. Your job? Follow the trail.

Pro Tip: Use active listening techniques, like repeating what the customer says in your own words. For example:

Customer: "We've had issues scaling our operations."

You: "So you're looking for a solution that grows with your business—did I get that right?"

- **The Authenticity Advantage**

Gen Z buyers have a built-in "BS detector." They'll sniff out insincerity faster than you can say, "limited time offer."

Pro Tip: Ditch the scripted pitches. Instead, share real stories or even failures where your product helped turn things around. People connect with people, not products.

Example: "Honestly, we had a client like you who was skeptical about our platform at first. But after two months, they cut their costs by 20%. Let me show you how they did it."

- **Simplify, Simplify, Simplify**

In a world of TikTok and 280-character tweets, no one has time for long-winded explanations.

Pro Tip: Boil your pitch down to a 10-second statement. If you can't explain the value in one sentence, you don't understand it well enough.

Example: "Our software helps you save time by automating 80% of your daily admin tasks."

- **AI Is a Tool, Not a Crutch**

Yes, AI is amazing, but it's not a substitute for emotional intelligence. Use it to analyze data, predict trends, or schedule follow-ups—but don't let it replace your intuition.

Pro Tip: Use AI to spot patterns (like which emails get the best response), but always add a personal touch. A quick "Hey, I noticed you liked our demo—let's chat more!" beats any automated template.

Modern Insights for Tackling Black Spots

- **Red Flag Radar**

Don't ignore the warning signs. If a prospect seems hesitant or their questions don't match their actions, dig deeper.

Pro Tip: Ask blunt but respectful questions.

- "Is there anything about this solution that doesn't feel like the right fit for you?"

- **Deliver (and Overdeliver)**

Overpromising is the fastest way to lose a deal—and your reputation. Be honest about what your product can and *can't* do.

Pro Tip: Under promise and then surprise them with added value. For example, include a free trial or bonus feature they didn't expect.

- **Follow Up Like a Friend**

Most deals are lost in the follow-up stage. Don't just send "checking in" emails—make your follow-ups meaningful.

Pro Tip: Send something helpful, like an article or a case study, and tie it to your conversation.

- "I remembered you mentioned scaling your operations—this article has some great tips. Let me know what you think!"

Flipping the Script: From Pitfalls to Power Plays

Here's the thing: Blind spots and black spots aren't just challenges—they're opportunities. Every time you miss a signal or hit a snag, it's a chance to learn and level up. The best salespeople don't avoid these shadows; they use them to shine.

Final Thought: Seeing the Shadows

Sales isn't just about closing deals, it's about opening doors. Blind spots teach you to see what you've missed. Black spots teach you to navigate with caution. Together, they make you a better, sharper, more empathetic seller. And in a digital world where authenticity is king, that's the real key to success.

Case Study: A Blind Spot Turned into a Visionary Success

Blind spots don't just exist in sales, they're everywhere, in business and in life. Sometimes, there are small oversights; other times, they're missing opportunities waiting to be seized. The following story is a real-life example of how one person identified a blind spot, took a bold step, and turned his passion into profit. It's a lesson in seeing what others overlook and transforming uncertainty into opportunity.

From Sales to Soccer:

Turning Passion into Profit

Business trips often bring unexpected encounters, but one trip to Ghana gave me a story that stayed with me—a story of passion, vision, and the courage to chase both.

It started on an ordinary evening when the local distributor invited me to join a casual soccer game. Among the players was a young man, modest but brimming with energy. During a break, he introduced himself as a former sales manager for the same food company I was visiting. He had spent five years in the role but left it all to follow an unconventional dream. What unfolded next was nothing short of inspirational.

The Spark of Passion

This young man was not just a former sales manager—he was a passionate soccer enthusiast. Growing up, he had always been drawn to the game, and over time, he started noticing an untapped potential: the incredible talent of young African players. These were kids from remote villages, often playing barefoot or with makeshift balls made of rolled-up socks. Yet their skill, determination, and raw talent rivaled any academy-trained athlete.

He saw an opportunity not just to change his own life, but to transform theirs as well. With this vision, he left his stable sales job and launched a small talent-scouting business. The goal? To find these hidden gems, train them, and connect them with European soccer clubs hungry for new talent.

Turning Vision into Reality

In a few months, he built his business from scratch. He would travel to Ghana's remote villages, spending hours watching street games and identifying young players with exceptional talent. Once he signed them, he provided them with professional training for six months, hiring seasoned coaches to polish their skills.

Then came the brilliance: he recorded high-quality videos of these players in action and sent them directly to European soccer clubs. The response was overwhelming. Teams were eager to snap up these young, talented players, offering contracts that changed not only the players' lives but also the scouts' fortunes.

One by one, these players—who once kicked balls made of socks— started signing deals with major clubs. With every success, his reputation grew, and so did his business. He was no longer just a salesperson, he was a game-changer, literally and figuratively.

The Lesson: Passion Meets Purpose

This story is more than a tale of career reinvention; it's a masterclass in how to merge passion with business acumen to create value for everyone involved.

- **Spot the Opportunity**

The former sales manager didn't stumble into success by chance. He saw a gap in the market—European clubs seeking raw talent—and connected it to a resource he knew existed in abundance: Africa's untapped soccer players. Whether in sales or life, the ability to identify and act on opportunities is a game-changer.

- **Solve Multiple Problems at Once**

By scouting and training players, he wasn't just building a business, he was creating brighter futures for young athletes who had little to no opportunities. At the same time, he was solving a pain point for clubs looking for fresh talent. Win-win scenarios are the hallmark of sustainable success.

- **Take Risks for What You Love**

Leaving a secure job for an uncertain dream isn't easy. But when passion drives you, the risks become part of the journey. His courage to step out of his comfort zone paid off—not only financially but emotionally, as he found fulfillment in doing what he loved.

The Power of Sales Skills in Any Field

Even though he left the corporate world, his sales background played a crucial role in his success:

- **Negotiation Skills:** Signing young players and dealing with European clubs required sharp negotiation tactics.
- **Storytelling:** The videos of players were more than just footage— they were crafted stories showcasing talent and potential.
- **Relationship Building:** His ability to connect with clubs and gain their trust came from years of experience building relationships in his sales career.

The Hidden Opportunity in Blind Spots

At first glance, this story might seem like a detour from sales, but it's actually a perfect example of how **blind spots and black spots shape our decisions**. The young talent scout had a blind spot in his corporate sales career—he was so focused on traditional success that he didn't see the bigger opportunity in his passion for soccer. But once he recognized it, he turned what others overlooked into a thriving business.

Just like in sales, **blind spots aren't always failures—they're often missed chances to innovate, pivot, and create something meaningful**. The key is to train yourself to see what others don't, question assumptions, and take an action on what could be.

"True success isn't about what you sell, it's about what you create. When passion meets purpose, the results are extraordinary, and everyone wins."

The Art of Standing Out: Emphasizing Your Value Proposition in the Age of AI and Digital Sales

Imagine walking through a bustling marketplace. Every stall is shouting, every vendor is pitching, and it feels like a sea of sameness. But in the physical world, at least the shelves are finite—you can see the options, compare, and decide. In today's **digital sales world**, however, the shelves are **endless**. Customers are lost in a vast ocean of options, with algorithms throwing product after product at them. The challenge isn't just about catching their attention, it's about cutting through the noise and making your value impossible to ignore.

The key to thriving in this infinite marketplace is delivering a value proposition so clear, unique, and tailored that it grabs your customer's focus and keeps it. But here's the twist: in this digital-first era, **AI, data, and digital tools** aren't just supporting players, they're the stars of the show. They're the secret weapon to help brands not only meet but exceed customer expectations.

Let's explore how sales teams can emphasize their distinct value propositions and how AI and digital tools are redefining what it means to sell effectively in a world with endless options.

What Is a Distinct Value Proposition (DVP)?

Your DVP is what makes your product or service *different and better*. It's the promise of what your customer gets from you that they can't get anywhere else. But in the digital world, where customers have endless options, a generic promise won't cut it. Your DVP must be:

1. **Relevant:** Solve a problem that matters to your customer.
2. **Unique:** Offer something your competitors can't.
3. **Provable:** Back your claims with evidence or data.

The AI Edge: How Technology Amplifies Your DVP

AI isn't just a tool—it's a superpower for sharpening your value proposition and delivering it to the right people at the right time. Here's how:

- **Personalization at Scale**

AI analyzes massive amounts of customer data—like preferences, behaviors, and purchase history—to craft personalized pitches that resonate deeply.

Example:

A skincare brand uses AI to create custom product recommendations for every customer. Instead of generic ads, customers see, *"This serum is perfect for your oily skin and works best in humid climates like yours."* The result? A 30% increase in conversions.

Why It Works:

Relevance is at the heart of a strong DVP. When customers feel understood, they're more likely to trust and buy.

- **Predictive Analytics**

AI doesn't just react to what customers do—it predicts what they'll need next. This allows brands to offer solutions before customers even realize they need them.

Example:

A fitness app notices a user skipping workouts and sends a motivational push notification offering a free personal training session. The timely nudge re-engages the user and builds loyalty.

Why It Works:

Anticipating customer needs demonstrates value beyond the product itself, reinforcing your DVP as a problem-solver.

- **Automation for Seamless Experiences**

AI-powered chatbots, CRM integrations, and automated follow-ups create smooth, hassle-free customer journeys.

Example:

An online retailer's AI chatbot answers customer queries instantly, recommends complementary products, and processes orders—all in one interaction. Shoppers are impressed by the convenience and come back for more.

Why It Works:

A seamless experience is part of your operational value. Customers value brands that make their lives easier.

- **Real-Time Feedback Loops**

AI tools monitor customer sentiment in real-time, helping sales teams adjust their approach on the fly.

Example:

During a virtual sales demo, AI detects hesitation in the customer's tone when discussing pricing. The salesperson adjusts their pitch to highlight ROI instead of cost, salvaging the deal.

Why It Works:

Adapting in real-time shows customers that your brand is agile and attuned to their concerns—both key drivers of trust.

Digital Tools: Enabling the Modern Sales Team

AI is just one piece of the puzzle. Digital tools and data analytics amplify a sales team's ability to deliver on their DVP. Here's how:

- **Omnichannel Presence**

Brands meet customers wherever they are—on social media, e-commerce platforms, or in-person events. Digital tools help integrate these touchpoints for a cohesive experience.

Example:

Nike's mobile app integrates shopping, workout plans, and exclusive offers, creating a one-stop-shop for active lifestyles.

- **Data-Driven Storytelling**

Numbers don't lie, but they're even better when paired with compelling stories. Data visualization tools help sales teams show—rather than tell—the value of their offering.

Example:

A SaaS company uses data dashboards to show prospects how much time and money they've wasted on outdated tools, making the case for switching to their platform.

- **Continuous Learning and Optimization**

Digital platforms provide insights into what works and what doesn't, enabling sales teams to refine their strategies.

Example:

A clothing brand A/B tests email campaigns, learning that messages with personalized styling tips outperform generic ones by 40%. The insights feed into their future campaigns.

Who's Already Winning with AI and Digital Sales?

- **Amazon**

Amazon's recommendation engine accounts for over **35% of its revenue**. By leveraging AI to predict what customers want, they've made convenience their ultimate DVP.

- **Sephora**

Sephora uses AI-powered beauty quizzes to offer tailored product suggestions, creating a highly personalized shopping experience that builds trust and drives loyalty.

- **Spotify**

Spotify's AI-driven playlists, like "Discover Weekly," are a masterclass in personalization. They turn users into loyal fans by consistently delivering relevant, unique, and delightful experiences.

The Gen Z Connection: Why This Matters

Gen Z buyers are digital natives who demand:

- **Personalization:** They want brands to treat them as individuals, not demographics.
- **Transparency:** They value authenticity and expect brands to back up their claims.
- **Seamlessness:** They don't have patience for clunky processes or outdated tech.

For sales teams targeting Gen Z, AI and digital tools are non-negotiable. They allow you to meet these expectations while standing out in a crowded marketplace.

Final Thought: AI and Digital Are the New Sales Frontier

In the race to win customers, brands that embrace AI and digital tools don't just sell—they lead. By amplifying your DVP with technology, you can deliver the right message, at the right time, to the right audience, creating meaningful connections that drive long-term value.

"In sales, the ultimate differentiator isn't just what you sell—it's how you sell it. AI, data, and digital tools turn a good pitch into a transformative experience, making your value proposition not just compelling but unforgettable."

Leveling Up: Playing the Long Game in Sales

In today's digital world, the biggest black spots in sales aren't just shady deals, they're outdated tactics, missed chances, and friction-filled buying experiences. Too many salespeople focus on quick wins, but the real game-changers think long-term. They don't just sell; they solve. They don't just pitch; they personalize.

Winning in sales today is like mastering chess, not checkers—it's about thinking ahead, spotting blind spots before they become roadblocks, and creating seamless, value-packed experiences that keep customers coming back. The stories ahead show exactly how strategic sales moves can turn rejection into innovation, transactions into partnerships, and struggling moments into your biggest wins.

Chess, Not Checkers: Mastering the Art of Strategic Sales

Sales is strategy, not sprinting. It's not about quick wins; it's about building something lasting, both for you and your client. To illustrate this, let's go deeper into the key points with stories that show why strategic thinking, embracing struggles, focusing on the client's value, and reshaping the buying process are game changers.

Struggling Moments: The Seed of Innovation

The Dropbox Story

Drew Houston, the founder of Dropbox, pitched his file-sharing solution to investors who shrugged it off. The feedback? "There's already plenty of ways to share files." Drew could've given up, but instead, he doubled down. He realized his problem wasn't building, the solution—it was showing people they had the problem. So, he created a now-iconic explainer video that went viral, demonstrating Dropbox's ease of use. The result? Thousands of signups before the product even launched.

In sales, rejection isn't the end; it's feedback. If a prospect says no, don't just take it personally, take it strategically. Are they struggling to see the value? Is there a way to reframe your pitch or use storytelling to make it resonate? Struggle forces you to innovate.

Personalization Through Struggle

Let's say you're selling a SaaS product, and a client says, "We don't have the budget." Instead of walking away, you dig deeper: Why is their budget tight? Maybe they're struggling with outdated systems that cost them more than they save. This insight lets you reposition your product—not as an expense but as a tool for cost reduction. Struggling moments force you to see the client's blind spots and turn them into growth opportunities.

Continuous Value: Making Clients Partners, Not Transactions

Amazon Prime Strategy

When Amazon launched Prime, it wasn't just about selling more products; it was about locking in continuous value for customers. For $99 a year, customers got free two-day shipping, exclusive content, and more. What Amazon really sold was convenience and loyalty. By making customers feel like they were constantly getting more value, they didn't just win a sale, they won a lifelong customer.

For a sales professional, this means looking beyond the immediate contract. For example, if you're selling software, don't stop at implementation. Offer ongoing training, quarterly check-ins to discuss ROI, or even exclusive beta access to new features. When clients see you as someone committed to their long-term success, they'll choose you every time, even over cheaper competitors.

A Fitness Example

Consider a gym selling memberships. A traditional approach might push discounts or special offers. A strategic approach thinks beyond the initial sale: How can the gym keep members engaged? Maybe it's by offering free wellness consultations, personalized workout plans, or access to a member-only community. This transforms the gym from a place to work out into a partner in members' health journeys.

The same applies to any sales role. Think about how your product or service becomes a continuous thread in your client's story.

Focus on Buying, Not Selling

The Warby Parker Approach

Warby Parker didn't reinvent glasses—they reinvented how people *bought* them. Before Warby Parker, buying glasses meant visiting an optometrist, dealing with high markups, and limited choices. Warby Parker flipped the script: they offered affordable, stylish frames online and let customers try them at home before purchasing. By simplifying the buying process and reducing friction, they turned a painful experience into an easy, even enjoyable one.

If you're in sales, think about your process. Is it simple? Transparent? Empathetic? Ask yourself, "What hurdles can I remove for the client?" Whether it's flexible payment terms, virtual product demos, or proactive support, small changes can make the buying experience smooth and empowering.

A Tech Buying Story

I once worked with a client who was frustrated by the complexity of purchasing enterprise software. Every vendor threw tech jargon at them and forced them to sit through endless demos. So, instead of following the crowd, I started with one question: "What's your biggest headache right now?" That shifted the conversation. They explained their team's inefficiency, and I tailored the demo to show exactly how my product solved their problem. They didn't just buy the software—they praised how easy the process was.

Think Five Moves Ahead

The Apple Ecosystem

Apple doesn't just sell iPhones; it creates an ecosystem. When you buy an iPhone, it's not just a phone, it's a gateway to Apple services, accessories, and other devices. Apple's goal isn't to sell a single product; it's to bring you into a world where every product and service feeds into the next.

Sales professionals can do the same by thinking long-term. Say you're selling a CRM. Instead of closing the deal and walking away, explore how the CRM can integrate with other systems, help the client's future expansion plans, or scale as their business grows. You're not just solving today's problem—you're solving problems they don't even know they'll have tomorrow.

Real Estate with Vision

In real estate, a forward-thinking agent doesn't just sell homes; they sell lifestyles. Imagine showing a young family a house. Instead of focusing on square footage, you point out the great school district, nearby parks, and family-friendly community events. You're not just selling a house; you're selling the client's future. The family isn't just buying a property—they're investing in their dream life.

Gen Z Salesperson: The Game-Changer

Leveraging Tech and Trends

Gen Z, this is your moment. With your tech-savviness, you can use AI to analyze client behavior, predict trends, and create hyper-personalized experiences. For instance, imagine using data analytics to anticipate when a client might need to restock your product and proactively reaching out with a tailored offer. That's not just sales, it's innovation.

Sustainability Sells

Today's buyers care about values as much as value. If your product or service aligns with sustainability, inclusivity, or innovation, lean into that. Show how your brand stands for more than just profits. Clients want to work with companies that share their values.

The Final Move

Sales is a chessboard. Every move—listening to your client, innovating through struggle, delivering continuous value, and focusing on their buying journey—is part of a bigger game. When you stop playing to win the deal and start playing to build a partnership, you'll find yourself mastering the art of strategic sales.

Remember, great sales isn't just about closing the deal—it's about opening a door to something much bigger.

CHAPTER 8

The Art of Happy Sales: Building Relationships in a Modern World

As we've discussed throughout this book, Sales has evolved. It's no longer about the loudest pitch or the flashiest suit. Today's sales are about empathy, connection, and authenticity. For Gen Z, who've grown up in a world of transparency and instant communication, the old-school sales tactics just don't cut it anymore. It's time to rewrite the rules. Welcome to Happy Sales—where everyone wins.

What Is Happy Sales?

Happy sales isn't just about closing deals; it's about creating an experience that leaves both the salesperson and the client feeling good about the interaction. It's about selling with integrity, building relationships, and focusing on long-term value over short-term wins.

Let's break it down:

- **Empathy over Aggression:** Understanding your client's needs rather than forcing your agenda.
- **Transparency over Tricks:** Being honest and clear, even if it means losing the sale.
- **Partnership over Pushiness:** Collaborating with clients to achieve shared goals.

Story: The Shoe Store That Changed the Game

Imagine a small shoe store struggling to compete with big online retailers. Instead of cutting prices to the bone or spamming customers with ads, the owner decided to focus on creating *happy sales.*

How? By focusing on the customer's experience. Every shopper who walked in was greeted warmly and offered a free foot analysis to ensure they found the perfect fit. Instead of upselling, the staff would ask, "What's your biggest challenge when it comes to shoes?" This question opened the door to real conversations.

One customer, a nurse who worked 12-hour shifts, shared her struggle with foot pain. The team didn't just sell her a pair of shoes; they offered recommendations for insoles and foot care routines. A week later, the nurse returned—not just for another pair, but with three coworkers in tow.

That's the power of happy sales: it creates advocates, not just customers.

The 3 Pillars of Happy Sales

1. Make It Personal

People don't want to be treated like numbers. They want to feel seen, heard, and valued. This means tailoring your approach to their unique needs.

Example: Spotify's Wrapped Campaign

Spotify doesn't just sell music streaming; it sells a personalized experience. Every year, it releases "Spotify Wrapped," a summary of users' listening habits. By showing people their favorite songs, artists, and even quirky stats (like how many minutes they've listened), Spotify creates a deep emotional connection with its users.

In sales, this could look like sending a client a personalized thank-you note, celebrating milestones with them, or remembering their preferences for future recommendations.

2. Focus on Joy, Not Just ROI

Yes, sales are about numbers, but they're also about emotions. When you create joy for your clients, you build trust and loyalty.

Story: The Coffee Shop That Gave More

A local coffee shop started giving out handwritten notes with every order. These weren't generic thank-you—they were little doses of positivity, like "You've got this!" or "The world is better with you in it." Customers began sharing the notes on social media, and the shop's popularity exploded.

What does this teach us? People remember how you make them feel. In sales, think about ways to surprise and delight your clients. Maybe it's a small freebie, a handwritten thank-you, or even just an unexpected follow-up call to check in—not to sell, but to say, "Hey, I'm here if you need anything."

3. **Sell Solutions, Not Products**

Today's buyers are savvy. They don't want to hear about product features; they want to know how you'll solve their problems.

Example: Tesla's Vision

When Tesla sells cars, it's not just selling a vehicle; it's selling a vision for a sustainable future. By focusing on what the product *does*—reducing carbon emissions, saving on fuel costs, and even providing a fun driving experience—they've turned customers into brand ambassadors.

In your sales process, ask yourself: "What problem am I solving?" Then, show your client how your solution fits into their life.

Gen Z and Happy Sales

Gen Z isn't just another customer base, they're redefining what sales success looks like. They prioritize sustainability, inclusivity, and authenticity, and they expect brands to do the same. To truly connect—whether as customers or team members—it's not about just selling to them but aligning with what matters to them.

Be Real

Fake smiles and rehearsed pitches won't work. Be genuine. Share your story, your struggles, and why you believe in what you're selling.

Use Tech Wisely

Gen Z loves tech, but they value human connections even more. Using tools like AI and CRM software to enhance your relationships—not replace them.

Lead with Purpose

If your product or service supports a cause or makes the world better, shout it from the rooftops. Gen Z wants to buy from brands that align with their values.

Story: Turning a Tough Client Around

A young sales rep, Mia, had been trying to close a deal with a tech company for months. Every meeting ended with the client saying, "We're not ready yet." Frustrated but determined, Mia decided to shift her approach.

Instead of pushing her product, she started asking more questions: What challenges were they facing? What was holding them back? She learned the company had just undergone a major restructuring and was overwhelmed.

Mia didn't pitch her product in the next meeting. Instead, she offered a free consultation to help them streamline their processes, no strings attached. The client was so impressed that they signed a six-figure deal two months later.

The lesson? Happy sales isn't about forcing a deal; it's about being there for your clients when they need you.

Sales today isn't just about transactions, it's about transformations. It's about creating moments of joy, solving real problems, and building relationships that last.

So, whether you're selling software, sneakers, or solar panels, remember this: The happiest salespeople aren't the ones chasing commissions, they're the ones building connections. Because when you make your clients happy, success is inevitable.

Welcome to the era of Happy Sales. Let's create something unforgettable together.

From Happy Sales to Happy Brands: Building a Legacy of Joy and Trust

It's not just salespeople who need to embrace the happy philosophy—brands must evolve, too. A happy brand is one that goes beyond products and services to create meaningful connections with its customers, employees, and communities. It's about becoming a source of trust, joy, and inspiration. In today's world, where authenticity and purpose are paramount, evolving into a happy brand isn't just a strategy, it's a necessity.

What Makes a Happy Brand?

A happy brand is one that:

1. **Delivers more than it promises:** It surprises and delights its audience.
2. **Values people over profits:** It cares about its customers, employees, and stakeholders.
3. **Aligns with purpose:** It stands for something bigger than sales and aligns its actions with its values.
4. **Fosters a sense of community:** It builds relationships, not just transactions.

Let's explore how brands can achieve this with real-world examples.

- ## Delivering More Than Expected: The Surprise Factor

Story: Chewy's Pet Customer Service

Chewy, the online pet retailer, is known for its exceptional customer service. One customer ordered dog food but later contacted Chewy to return it after their dog passed away. Not only did Chewy process the refund, but they also sent flowers, and a handwritten condolence note.

Chewy didn't have to do this, but by exceeding expectations, they created a customer for life—not to mention a viral story that showcased their values.

Lesson for Brands: Surprise your customers with thoughtful gestures. Whether it's a thank-you note, a small freebie, or going the extra mile in service, these moments of unexpected kindness transform your brand from a vendor into a companion.

- ## Putting People Over Profits: Building Trust

Story: Patagonia's Bold Move

Patagonia is the poster child of a happy brand. Known for its environmental activism, the company once ran an ad with the headline: *"Don't Buy This Jacket."* The campaign encouraged consumers to repair old clothes rather than buying new ones, a move that seemed counterintuitive for a retail brand. But Patagonia's commitment to sustainability struck a chord with its audience, boosting both its sales and its reputation.

Lesson for Brands: Don't be afraid to stand by your values, even if it seems risky. Customers respect brands that prioritize people and the planet over short-term profits.

- ## Aligning with Purpose: The Heart of a Happy Brand

Story: TOMS Shoes

TOMS pioneered the "One for One" model: for every pair of shoes sold, the company donates a pair to someone in need. This simple yet powerful mission resonated with socially conscious consumers and turned TOMS into a global brand.

Today's customers, especially Gen Z—want to support brands that make a difference. They're not just buying a product; they're buying into a cause.

Lesson for Brands: Identify your purpose and bake it into everything you do, from your marketing campaigns to your internal culture. Your purpose should inspire your team and excite your customers.

- ## Creating a Community: Fostering Belonging

Story: Starbucks Third Place Philosophy

Starbucks doesn't just sell coffee; it creates a "third place" where people feel comfortable to work, meet, or relax. The brand has cultivated a sense of community through its welcoming atmosphere, personalized service (hello, custom drink names!), and initiatives like their app-based rewards program.

Starbucks' success isn't just about the coffee; it's about the emotional connection it creates with customers.

Lesson for Brands: Create spaces—physical or digital—where your customers feel like they belong. This could be through social media communities, loyalty programs, or local events. A brand that fosters connection becomes indispensable.

- ## Innovating for Joy: Keeping It Fresh

Story: LEGO's Reinvention

LEGO is more than a toy; it's a brand that sparks creativity and joy for all ages. Facing financial struggles in the early 2000s, LEGO reinvented itself by collaborating with franchises like *Star Wars* and *Harry Potter*, launching digital games, and creating the LEGO Movie. This evolution transformed LEGO into a cultural icon.

Lesson for Brands: Never stop innovating. Look for ways to keep your offerings fresh, exciting, and relevant to your audience's evolving tastes.

Becoming a Happy Brand: Practical Steps

Start Inside Out:

A happy brand starts with happy employees. Invest in your team by fostering a positive workplace culture, offering opportunities for growth, and recognizing their contributions. Happy employees create happy customers.

Listen and Adapt:

Engage with your audience. Use surveys, social media, and feedback loops to understand what your customers want and how you can serve them better.

Build Emotional Connections:

Don't just sell a product—tell a story. Show how your brand fits into your customers' lives and helps them achieve their goals or solve their problems.

Celebrate Successes:

Share your wins with your customers and community. Whether it's reaching a sustainability milestone or launching a new initiative, celebrate it in a way that involves your audience.

Be Transparent:

Honesty builds trust. Share your journey, challenges, and plans openly with your customers. When people feel included in your story, they root for your success.

A Happy Brand in Action: Apple's Genius Bar

Apple doesn't just sell gadgets; it creates experiences. The Genius Bar isn't just tech support, it's a space where customers feel empowered to learn and grow. Apple's focus on customer education, seamless product integration, and beautifully designed stores reinforces its status as a happy brand.

The result? Apple customers don't just buy products; they become lifelong fans.

Closing Thought: The Ripple Effect of Happiness

When you evolve into a happy brand, you don't just sell products, you create ripples of joy, trust, and loyalty that spread far and wide. Happy brands inspire employees, delight customers, and make a positive impact on the world.

As you build your brand, remember this: happiness is contagious. The more you give, the more you receive. And in today's world, where authenticity and connection matter more than ever, being a happy brand isn't just good for business, it's the only way forward.

Let's make happiness the cornerstone of every brand. After all, the happiest brands create the most loyal fans.

CHAPTER 9

The New B2B Playbook: Selling in the Digital-First Era

B2B sales is no longer stuck in the past. The game has changed, and buyers now expect the same speed, convenience, and personalization they get in B2C. If your sales strategy still relies on clunky processes and outdated playbooks, you're already falling behind.

Winning today means ditching the old-school hustle and embracing a smarter, more agile approach. This chapter breaks down four game-changing strategies that are shaping the future of B2B sales— seamless multi-channel experiences, flexible tech, smart automation, and recurring revenue models. These aren't just trends; they're the blueprint for thriving in a world where buyers call the shots.

It's time to level up. Let's go.

1. Seamless Multi-Channel Selling

In today's world, buyers move between channels faster than you can say "conversion funnel." They might research online, consult with a rep, and then complete the purchase in a mobile app. Your job is to make their journey smooth.

- Example: A chemical supplier noticed that clients were using their website to browse products but preferred calling reps to close deals. By linking their eCommerce portal with their CRM, they created a unified experience where reps could see exactly what buyers were browsing and step in with personalized offers.

Practical Tip: Align your online and offline sales channels. Make sure your sales team knows what customers are doing online and vice versa. Tools like Salesforce Commerce Cloud can help.

2. Flexible Sales Tech Setups

"Headless" systems sound like something from a horror movie, but they're actually a tech dream. These setups let businesses tweak the front-end customer experience (think design and functionality) without breaking the back-end operations.

- Example: A B2B furniture company wanted to refresh their website's look without disrupting their supply chain integrations. A headless system let them roll out a sleek, mobile-friendly design in weeks, not months, while keeping their inventory and logistics humming along.

Practical Tip: If you're building or upgrading your eCommerce platform, look into headless options like Shopify Plus or BigCommerce. They're scalable and adaptable, perfect for the fast-changing B2B landscape.

3. Open Systems and APIs

Gone are the days when sales tools were siloed and clunky. Open systems powered by APIs let you connect everything—CRM, eCommerce, ERP, you name it—into one harmonious machine.

- Example: A medical supply company connected their eCommerce store to their inventory system via APIs. When a buyer places an order, the system checks stock in real-time, sends a confirmation, and schedules delivery—all automatically.

Practical Tip: Talk to your tech team about integrating APIs into your sales tools. The goal is to automate as much as possible while keeping everything connected.

4. Subscription Models

Why sell once when you can sell every month? Subscription-based models are taking over B2B because they offer predictable revenue for sellers and ongoing value for buyers.

- Example: An IT services firm switched from one-time software sales to a subscription model, bundling updates and support. Customers loved the flexibility, and the company's revenue stabilized with recurring payments.

Practical Tip: Think about whether your product or service could be offered as a subscription. Even traditional industries (like manufacturing) are finding ways to adapt to this model.

Maximizing Subscription Models for Long-Term Success

Subscription-based models aren't just about predictable revenue, they're about building deeper, long-term relationships with customers. In the new B2B world, businesses that offer ongoing value and seamless experiences will dominate the market. Here's how to adapt your sales strategy to make the most of this shift.

How to Win in the New B2B World

1. Invest in eCommerce:
   Build a user-friendly platform that lets buyers research, compare, and purchase with minimal friction.

2. Empower Buyers:
    Offer self-service options for simple transactions but keep your
    sales team ready to step in for complex deals.

3. Think Like B2C:
    Borrow strategies from successful B2C brands, like personalized
    recommendations, mobile-first design, and fast delivery options.

4. Train Your Team:
    Your sales team's role is changing. Train them to become
    trusted advisors who complement the digital buying journey,
    not compete with it.

5. Stay Agile:
    The digital landscape changes fast. Stay flexible with your tools
    and processes to adapt to new trends and technologies.

The line between B2B and B2C is blurring, and eCommerce is at
the heart of this shift. Buyers want the ease and speed of consumer
platforms in their professional purchases. By embracing these changes
and investing in digital tools, you can turn this transformation into a
massive opportunity.

5. Selling Complex and Custom Products: When "One Size Fits All" Doesn't Cut It

Gone are the days when customers settled for cookie-cutter products.
Today's buyers want things their way—whether they're ordering sneakers,
furniture, or industrial equipment. And they're willing to pay more for
it. According to Deloitte, over 50% of consumers prefer customized
products, and this B2C trend is quickly reshaping the B2B landscape.

In this era of personalization, sales teams have to adapt. It's not just about
pitching a standard solution anymore, it's about understanding every

little detail of your customer's needs and delivering something that feels tailor-made for them.

Here's how companies are stepping up their game—and how you can too.

Why Customization is the New Standard

Think about it: Would you buy a car that only came in one color or a house with no options for upgrades? Probably not. Buyers today expect the same level of flexibility with everything they purchase.

Real-World Story: The $50,000 Helmet

Take Xenith, a company that makes custom football helmets. Their customers—athletes and teams—demand not just protection but precision. Using advanced Configure, Price, Quote (CPQ) software, Xenith allows teams to design helmets tailored to their exact specifications. The result? A premium product that commands premium pricing and delivers unbeatable customer satisfaction.

Lesson: Customization isn't just a nice-to-have anymore, it's a competitive edge.

The Secret Weapon: CPQ Software

What is CPQ?

CPQ stands for Configure, Price, Quote. It's software that helps sales teams:

- Build complex product configurations in real time.
- Generate accurate quotes instantly.
- Streamline the entire sales process from design to delivery.

Think of CPQ as your backstage pass to creating custom products without the chaos. By connecting to CRM, ERP, and design tools, CPQ turns customization into a smooth, scalable process.

Real-World Example: NanaWall's Transformation

NanaWall, a company specializing in custom glass wall systems, integrated CPQ software into their sales process. Instead of spending hours—or days—manually configuring products and calculating costs, their reps could now generate quotes in minutes. This led to faster deals, happier customers, and higher revenue.

Practical Tip: If you're selling custom products, invest in CPQ software like Epicor CPQ or Salesforce CPQ. It'll save you time, reduce errors, and give your clients an unmatched buying experience.

Next-Level Selling with AR and VR

Customization isn't just about specs—it's about visualization. Customers don't want to guess how their custom product will look; they want to see it, experience it, and interact with it. Enter augmented reality (AR) and virtual reality (VR).

How AR and VR Are Changing the Game

a. Visualizing Products in Real-Time

    AR overlays digital images onto the real world, letting customers see how a product will fit into their space.

    o   Example: Wayfair's "View in Room" feature lets shoppers visualize furniture in their homes using AR. This one tool boosted their conversions fivefold.

b. Customizing in 3D

VR transports buyers to virtual environments where they can tweak products in real-time.

> o   Example: A heavy machinery company used VR to let clients explore and modify equipment in a digital showroom. Clients loved the hands-on experience, and sales soared.

c. Interactive Training

AR and VR aren't just for selling—they're for teaching. These tools help clients understand how to use complex products before they even buy them.

> o   Example: A medical device company used AR to train surgeons on their tools, leading to increased trust and higher sales.

How to Bring It All Together

Here's where things get really exciting: CPQ + AR/VR = Magic.

Imagine this: A customer is designing a custom product using CPQ software. With AR, they can see the product in their office, factory, or home before buying. With VR, they can walk through a virtual showroom and make changes on the fly.

Real-World Inspiration:

A luxury yacht company combined CPQ with VR to let clients design their dream boats. Clients could walk through virtual models, choose materials, and customize layouts. The result? More sales—and more satisfied customers.

Practical Tip: Look for CPQ software that integrates AR and VR capabilities. It's an investment that'll wow your customers and make complex products feel approachable.

Why Gen Z Will Love This

Gen Z buyers and decision-makers grew up with apps, gaming, and instant gratification. They expect seamless, visually engaging, and interactive experiences in their purchasing journeys. Selling to them? Show don't tell.

- Shareable Moments: Use AR/VR to create "wow" moments they'll talk about online.
- Transparency Wins: Show them every customization option upfront. No surprises.

Selling complex and custom products isn't about complexity, it's about clarity. The right tools, like CPQ and AR/VR, make customization easy, exciting, and accessible. As buyer expectations continue to rise, the companies that embrace these technologies will set themselves apart.

6. Customer Experience and Retention: Keep Them Coming Back for More

Let's be real: Sales don't stop at "Congratulations, we closed the deal!" That's just the warm-up. In today's competitive world, it's all about what happens next. Smart businesses know that keeping a customer is way more valuable (and cheaper) than chasing down new ones. The secret? Delivering a customer experience (CX) that's so good, they can't imagine doing business anywhere else.

The Power of Experience

Here's a wild stat: 90% of customers are more likely to repurchase after a positive service experience. Even more impressive, companies that prioritize CX report 60% higher profits than those that don't. Why? Because customers don't just buy products—they buy relationships, trust, and vibes.

Story: The $40 Latte That Turned a Customer Into a Fan

Picture this: A customer orders a latte from a local coffee shop using their app. The order gets mixed up, and they end up with a black coffee instead. Annoyed, they left a review. Within an hour, the manager reaches out, apologizing and offering a $40 gift card as an apology.

What started as a negative experience turned into a story the customer couldn't stop telling their friends about. They didn't just remain customers, they became fans.

Lesson: Every interaction, good or bad, is a chance to strengthen your relationship with the customer.

Why Retention Beats Acquisition

a.   Retention Drives Profits

Bump up your customer retention by just 5%, and your profits could soar by 25% to 95%. Plus, keeping an existing customer costs five times less than finding a new one.

- Real-World Example: Apple doesn't just sell you an iPhone; they keep you coming back with iCloud, Apple Music, and seamless updates. Their ecosystem locks customers in by making it inconvenient—and frankly, unappealing—to leave.

Practical Tip: Think about ways to create stickiness in your product or service. Loyalty programs, exclusive perks, or seamless integrations work wonders.

b. Loyal Customers Become Advocates

Happy customers don't just buy more, they sell for you. They share their experiences on social media, leave glowing reviews, and bring in their friends.

- Example: Look at Glossier, a beauty brand that turned its customers into influencers. By engaging with their community and listening to feedback, Glossier created products that customers felt personally connected to—and they shared that love online.

Practical Tip: Encourage your customers to share their experiences. Offer incentives for reviews or referrals and always respond to feedback—good or bad.

How to Level Up Your Customer Experience

a. Delight at Every Touchpoint

The journey doesn't end at checkout. Post-purchase follow-ups personalized thank-you, and stellar support are what keep customers coming back.

- Example: Chewy, an online pet retailer, sends handwritten notes to customers and even flowers when a pet passes away. It's those small, thoughtful touches that create lifelong loyalty.

Practical Tip: Create a post-sale engagement plan. Check in with customers after their purchase, offer helpful tips, or send a surprise discount for their next order.

b. **Use Data to Stay Ahead**

Retention isn't just about reacting—it's about anticipating. AI and data analytics can help you spot trends, predict issues, and even recommend solutions before customers know they need them.

- Example: Spotify uses data to create personalized playlists like "Discover Weekly," keeping users engaged and excited about their service.

Practical Tip: Invest in tools like Zendesk or HubSpot to analyze customer data and uncover patterns. Use this info to tailor your communication and fix pain points proactively.

c. **Listen and Evolve**

Customers are your best source of feedback. Pay attention to what they're saying—online and offline—and use it to improve.

- Example: A SaaS company noticed users were frustrated with a confusing feature. Instead of ignoring it, they revamped the interface and rolled out an update. Users felt heard, and retention rates spiked.

Practical Tip: Regularly survey your customers, monitor reviews, and set up a system to act on their feedback. Even small tweaks can make a big difference.

Why Gen Z Cares About CX

Gen Z isn't just a buyer, they're a movement. They value transparency, empathy, and experiences that feel personal and meaningful. To win their loyalty, brands need to go beyond "service" and create an emotional connection.

- Be Authentic: Gen Z can spot fake sincerity a mile away. Be real and own your mistakes.
- Be Accessible: Offer customer support on platforms they actually use, like social media or live chat.
- Be Thoughtful: Surprise them with small, meaningful gestures.

In sales, closing the deal is just step one. If you're serious about building a sustainable business, the real work starts after the handshake. Focus on creating unforgettable experiences, and you'll turn one-time buyers into lifelong fans who'll keep coming back—and bring their friends with them.

7- Sales and Marketing Alignment: The Ultimate Power Couple

Sales and marketing don't have to be frenemies anymore. When these two teams work together, the results can be magic. Aligned sales and marketing teams don't just hit their numbers, they smash them. Studies show that businesses with tightly aligned sales and marketing functions see a 36% boost in customer retention and a 38% jump in sales win rates.

But here's the kicker: Aligned teams also grew revenue 24% faster over three years. That's what happens when you stop playing tug-of-war and start pulling in the same direction.

Why Alignment Matters

Think of sales and marketing like a band. Sales is the lead singer, closing deals and bringing in fans. Marketing is the guitarist, setting the vibe and drawing the crowd in. When they're on the same wavelength, the performance is unforgettable. When they're not? Well, let's just say nobody's buying tickets.

- Marketing generates leads.

- Sales converts those leads.
- Together, they guide customers through a seamless journey.

When these roles overlap and collaborate, you don't just attract customers, you keep them for life.

Story: The Campaign That Clicked

A SaaS startup struggled to get their sales team excited about marketing leads. The reps said the leads weren't qualified, and marketing felt like sales wasn't following up effectively. Cue a brainstorming session where both teams worked together to define their ideal customer profile (ICP).

Marketing adjusted their campaigns to focus on ICPs, while sales agreed to follow up on every lead within 24 hours. Within three months, lead conversion rates doubled, and both teams finally felt like they were on the same team.

Lesson: Alignment starts with communication. When sales and marketing agree on what success looks like, everyone wins.

How Technology Bridges the Gap

The secret to sales and marketing harmony? Tech that talks to itself.

When your CRM, marketing automation tools, CPQ, and ERP systems work together, you eliminate silos and create a seamless flow of data. Here's how each tool plays its part:

a. **CRM: The Customer Tracker**

CRM (Customer Relationship Management) systems like Salesforce or HubSpot track every interaction a prospect has with your brand. Sales reps can see which emails a lead opened, what pages they visited, and what products caught their eye.

- Practical Tip: Use your CRM to identify hot leads based on engagement. Marketing can create nurture campaigns, and sales can strike when the iron's hot.

b. Marketing Automation: The Campaign Driver

Tools like Marketo or Mailchimp automate lead generation and nurture campaigns, ensuring prospects are warmed up before sales steps in.

- Real-World Example: A B2B logistics company used marketing automation to send personalized content based on a prospect's browsing history. By the time sales reached out, leads already knew the brand and were ready to talk.

c. CPQ: The Quote Creator

When it's time to seal the deal, Configure, Price, Quote (CPQ) software ensures accurate quotes and configurations. No more back-and-forth over pricing errors or availability issues.

- Practical Tip: Link your CPQ to your CRM so sales can pull quotes directly from customer data.

d. ERP: The Backbone

ERP (Enterprise Resource Planning) systems handle inventory, finance, and order fulfillment. By connecting ERP with your sales and marketing tools, everyone stays informed about stock levels and delivery timelines.

- Real-World Example: A manufacturing company integrated their ERP with their CRM and CPQ. When marketing launched a campaign for a new product, sales could instantly see inventory levels and delivery timelines, avoiding overpromising.

The Magic of Integration

When all these tools work together, you get an ecosystem that:

- Breaks down silos: Everyone—from sales to marketing to ops—works from the same data.
- Reduces errors: Real-time information means fewer mistakes and miscommunications.
- Improves CX: Customers enjoy faster, more accurate service.

Real-World Story: The Seamless Sales Funnel

An eCommerce company connected their CRM, marketing automation, and ERP systems. Here's how it worked:

- Marketing ran a campaign highlighting their top-selling product.
- Leads entered the CRM, where sales reps could see exactly which ads they'd clicked on.
- When a deal closed, ERP updated inventory automatically.

This alignment cut order processing time by 50% and boosted customer satisfaction scores.

How Gen Z Fits In

Gen Z is all about collaboration, transparency, and seamless experiences. If you want to win over these digital natives as customers—or hire them for your sales and marketing team alignment is non-negotiable.

- Transparency Wins: Show how marketing and sales work together for the greater good.
- Tech Is Life: Gen Z expects smooth integrations and hates clunky processes.

- Team Spirit: Highlight collaboration as part of your company culture.

Steps to Get Aligned

a. Define Shared Goals: Agree on what success looks like, whether it's lead quality, conversion rates, or revenue targets.
b. Meet Regularly: Weekly syncs between sales and marketing ensure everyone's on the same page.
c. Share Data: Use integrated tools to make sure both teams have access to the same information.
d. Celebrate Wins Together: When a big campaign crushes its goals, celebrate as a team.

When sales and marketing alien, it's like flipping the turbo switch on your business. Leads flow more smoothly, customers stick around longer, and revenue grows faster. In today's connected world, no team can afford to go it alone. So sync up, link your tools, and watch the magic happen.

8. Ethical and Sustainable Selling: The Future is Green

Imagine walking into a store and seeing two identical products on the shelf. One has a label that says, "Sustainably Sourced and Fair Trade Certified." The other? Nothing. Which one do you buy?

If you're like most consumers today, the choice is obvious. 88% of buyers want brands to help them make a positive impact, and many are willing to pay a premium to do it. For sales teams, this isn't just a nice-to-have—it's the new way to win hearts, wallets, and loyalty.

Why Ethical Selling Matters

Ethical and sustainable selling isn't just about ticking a box; it's about showing your customers that you care about the same things they do—protecting the planet, supporting workers, and building a better future. And here's the kicker: people are willing to pay for it. Buyers will shell out 9.4% more for products that are sustainably sourced and ethically produced.

Story: The $100 Sustainable Hoodie

Ever heard of Patagonia? Of course you have. They don't just sell outdoor gear—they sell a mission. When you buy a $100 hoodie from Patagonia, you're not just buying a hoodie. You're supporting fair labor practices, environmental conservation, and a company that promises to repair your hoodie for life.

This approach isn't just good for the planet, it's good for business. Customers love the story and feel proud to be part of something bigger.

Lesson: People don't just want products, they want to feel like they're making a difference. Give them that, and they'll choose you every time.

How to Sell Ethically and Sustainably

a.   Be a Storyteller, Not a Salesperson

Today's buyers care about *how* your product is made, not just *what* it does. Where do your materials come from? Are your workers treated fairly? How are you reducing your carbon footprint?

- Example: A chocolate company shared a behind-the-scenes video of their fair-trade cocoa farmers and sustainable packaging process. Customers loved the transparency, and sales skyrocketed.

Practical Tip: Add a sustainability or ethics section to your website and sales materials. Make it easy for your customers to understand the positive impact of their purchase.

b. Offer Transparency, Not Greenwashing

Transparency builds trust. Greenwashing—making empty claims about sustainability—destroys it. If you say your product is eco-friendly, back it up with certifications, data, and proof.

- Example: Allbirds, a sustainable shoe brand, shares a carbon footprint score for every product they sell. They also outline exactly how they offset emissions.

Practical Tip: Use tools like Carbon Trust to calculate and communicate the environmental impact of your products.

c. Make Ethics a Part of the Pitch

Don't just mention sustainability as an afterthought—make it central to your sales strategy. Talk about the impact of buying your product and how it aligns with your customer's values.

- Example: A furniture retailer offered a tree-planting initiative where every purchase funded reforestation effort. The campaign resonated with eco-conscious buyers, boosting sales and creating a deeper connection with their audience.

Practical Tip: Tie your product to a cause. Whether it's donating a percentage of profits or supporting a specific initiative, show customers the bigger picture.

d. Invest in Real Impact

Ethical selling starts with action. If your company isn't already taking steps toward sustainability and ethical practices, now is the time to start.

- Example: Ikea committed to becoming climate positive by 2030, and they're well on their way with solar-powered stores and recyclable products. Customers see this commitment and reward it with loyalty.

Practical Tip: Start small. Reduce waste, switch to sustainable packaging, or partner with ethical suppliers. Every step counts.

Why Gen Z is Leading the Charge

Gen Z doesn't just want products—they want purpose. They expect brands to align with their values and won't hesitate to call out companies that fall short.

- Authenticity is Everything: Gen Z hates fake vibes. If you're going to talk the talk, make sure you walk the walk.
- Social media is the Stage: Share your ethical journey on Instagram, TikTok, and LinkedIn. Show the behind-the-scenes effort, not just the polished final product.
- Make Them Proud to Buy: Gen Z wants to feel like their money is making a difference. Give them a reason to say, "I support this brand."

Steps to Go Ethical and Sustainable

a. Audit Your Processes: Identify areas where you can improve sustainability and ethical practices.
b. Partner with Good Players: Work with suppliers and organizations that share your values.
c. Train Your Sales Team: Equip your team with the stories, stats, and certifications they need to sell ethically.
d. Celebrate Milestones: Share your progress with your customers. It's a journey, and they'll appreciate your honesty.

Final Thought

Ethical and sustainable selling isn't a trend—it's the future. By aligning your sales approach with these values, you're not just selling a product. You're building a movement, creating impact, and earning loyalty from customers who care about making the world a better place.

9. Hyper-Personalization: The Future of Sales is Tailor-Made

Let's get real—nobody likes being treated like just another number. Whether it's in a text, a product recommendation, or a sales pitch, personalization isn't just nice to have anymore, it's what people *expect*. In a world where every ad, email, and playlist seems tailor-made for you, hyper-personalization is taking over sales, and the brands that get it right are winning big.

What is Hyper-Personalization?

Hyper-personalization is next-level personalization. It's not just calling someone by their first name in an email—it's using data, AI, and analytics to create a custom experience for every single buyer. Think Netflix knowing exactly what you want to watch or Spotify creating a playlist that feels like it was made just for you.

In sales, hyper-personalization means understanding your customer so well that you can anticipate their needs before they even know what they want.

Story: The Coffee Shop That Knows You

Imagine walking into your favorite coffee shop. Before you even say a word, the barista smiles and says, "Morning, Alex. Double-shot oat latte, right?"

That's not just good service, it's personalization. And now imagine your online shopping or B2B buying experience feels just like that. That's the power of hyper-personalization.

Why Hyper-Personalization Matters

Here's the tea: 80% of consumers are more likely to buy from a brand that offers personalized experiences. But it's not just about driving sales, it's about building relationships. When you show your customers that you *get* them, they trust you, stick with you, and become lifelong fans.

How Hyper-Personalization is Transforming Sales

a. Tailored Product Recommendations

Have you ever shopped on Amazon and seen, "People like you bought this?" That's hyper-personalization in action. By analyzing your browsing and buying habits, companies can suggest products you're most likely to love.

- Example: A sports retailer noticed a customer browsing running shoes. Instead of sending a generic email, they followed up with recommendations for marathon gear, like hydration packs and energy gels. The result? A 40% higher conversion rate.

Practical Tip: Use tools like Dynamic Yield or Salesforce Einstein to recommend products based on customer behavior.

b. Personalized Outreach

Nobody likes a cookie-cutter sales pitch. Hyper-personalization allows you to craft outreach messages that speak directly to a prospect's pain points and goals.

- Example: A software company used LinkedIn data to discover that a prospect's company was hiring remote workers. They customized their pitch to highlight how their product could streamline remote team management. The deal closed in record time.

Practical Tip: Research your prospects before reaching out. Mention something specific—like a recent company achievement or a shared connection—to show you've done your homework.

c. Customized Pricing and Offers

Hyper-personalization doesn't stop at recommendations, it extends to pricing. By analyzing a customer's buying history, preferences, and industry trends, sales teams can create offers that feel tailor-made.

- Example: A SaaS company analyzed user behavior and offered discounts on underutilized features to encourage higher engagement. Not only did the customer stick around—they upgraded.

Practical Tip: Use tools like PROS or Zilliant to create dynamic pricing strategies based on real-time data.

d. Real-Time Engagement

With AI and automation, you can interact with customers in the moment, responding to their actions as they happen.

- Example: An online retailer noticed a customer abandoning their cart. Within minutes, the customer received a personalized email: "Hi Emily, we saw you checking out that leather jacket. Here's 10% off to make it yours!" Emily completed the purchase that day.

Practical Tip: Set up triggers in your CRM or marketing tools to send real-time messages based on customer behavior.

Gen Z and Hyper-Personalization

Gen Z lives for experiences that feel *made for them.* They expect brands to know their vibe without being creepy about it. Here's how to win them over:

- Keep It Real: Personalization isn't about spamming—it's about relevance. If it feels forced or fake, they'll bounce.
- Go Beyond Basics: "Hey [First Name]" isn't enough. Dive deeper into their interests, behaviors, and needs.
- Use Their Favorite Platforms: Gen Z hangs out on Instagram, TikTok, and Snapchat. If you're not there, you're missing out.

How to Get Started with Hyper-Personalization

a. Leverage Data: Use analytics tools to understand customer behavior and preferences.
b. Invest in AI: AI tools like ChatGPT or HubSpot can help you craft personalized content and recommendations.
c. Segment Smartly: Group your customers based on shared traits or behaviors for easier personalization.
d. Test and Refine: Not every strategy will hit home. Experiment and use feedback to improve.

Hyper-personalization is the future of sales. It's about ditching the one-size-fits-all approach and treating every customer like they're your only customer. By leveraging data and AI, you can create experiences that are not just personal but unforgettable.

10- The Rise of AI in Emotional Selling: Tech with a Heart

We've all heard it: "People buy on emotion and justify with logic." But how do you tap into those emotions when you're selling through a screen or pitching to a data-driven buyer? Enter AI in emotional selling, the game-changer making sales feel more human—even when powered by machines.

AI is no longer just about crunching numbers or predicting trends. It's learning to understand human emotions and using that insight to help sales teams connect on a deeper level. From analyzing a prospect's tone to tailoring pitches that resonate emotionally, AI is giving sales a heart.

What is Emotional Selling?

Emotional selling is about connecting with your customers' feelings—whether that's excitement, trust, or solving a pain point that's been keeping them up at night. Now, AI is stepping in to help sales teams read the room (or the email) and respond in ways that feel authentic and empathetic.

Story: The AI That Saved a Deal

Meet James, a sales rep at a SaaS company struggling to close a deal. He hops on a video call with a potential client, but things feel... off. The client's tone is reserved, and their body language is guarded.

Thankfully, James is using AI-powered emotional analysis software. During the call, the tool flags that the client seems hesitant about pricing but interested in the product's long-term ROI. Armed with this insight, James pivots the conversation to focus on cost savings over time.

The result? A deal saved—and a happy client.

Lesson: Emotional selling isn't just about reading emotions; it's about responding to them in real time.

How AI Enhances Emotional Selling

1. Analyzing Sentiment in Real Time

AI tools can analyze tone, word choice, and even facial expressions during calls or emails. If a prospect sounds frustrated or hesitant, the AI alerts you so you can adjust your approach.

- Example: Tools like Cogito analyze voice patterns during sales calls, providing real-time coaching to reps on how to build rapport or ease tension.

Practical Tip: Try sentiment analysis tools to refine your communication strategy. They're like having a sales coach whispering in your ear.

2. **Crafting Emotionally Resonant Content**

AI can help create pitches, emails, and proposals that hit the emotional sweet spot. By analyzing past interactions, it can suggest language and themes that are most likely to resonate with a specific prospect.

- Example: A car dealership used AI to analyze customer preferences and sent personalized messages like, "Picture yourself on a road trip in your dream SUV." Conversion rates? Through the roof.

Practical Tip: Use AI tools like Jasper or Grammarly for emotionally tailored copywriting.

3. Identifying Customer Pain Points

AI doesn't just tell you what your prospects are feeling, it tells you *why*. By analyzing customer data, it highlights common frustrations or desires, so you can address them head-on.

- Example: A fitness app used AI to identify that many users dropped off after struggling with the meal-planning feature. By focusing their pitch on new, simplified meal plans, they boosted subscriptions by 25%.

Practical Tip: Use AI-powered analytics to dig into customer behavior and adjust your messaging accordingly.

4. Predicting Emotional Trends

AI doesn't just look at individual buyers—it spots patterns across your customer base. If it detects a growing frustration with delivery times, for example, it can flag this trend before it becomes a bigger problem.

- Example: An eCommerce company's AI noticed a spike in complaints about delayed shipping. The sales team preemptively reached out to assure customers their orders were on track, turning a potential PR disaster into a trust-building moment.

Practical Tip: Keep an eye on AI-driven trend reports to stay ahead of customer emotions and market shifts.

Gen Z and Emotional AI

Gen Z buyers value authenticity, empathy, and relevance. AI's ability to personalize and adapt in real time makes it a perfect fit for connecting with this generation.

- Real Feels Only: Gen Z hates robotic responses. AI tools that analyze emotions and respond authentically hit the mark.
- Efficiency with Heart: AI helps sales teams deliver fast responses without sacrificing emotional depth.
- Values Matter: Gen Z wants to feel like brands *get* them. AI can tailor messages that align with their goals and values.

How to Get Started with Emotional AI

1. Invest in Emotional Analytics Tools: Start with platforms like Cogito or Symbl.ai that analyze emotions during calls or chats.
2. Train Your Team: Emotional AI is a tool—not a replacement for empathy. Teach your team how to use insights to connect meaningfully.
3. Experiment with Personalization: Use AI to test different tones and styles in your outreach and see what clicks.
4. Monitor Trends: Regularly review the emotional data AI provides to fine-tune your strategy.

Chapter Wrap-Up: The Future of Sales is Human + AI

AI isn't here to replace the human side of sales, it's here to supercharge it. The smartest sales teams aren't choosing between tech and emotion; they're blending both to create deeper, more meaningful connections. Data + empathy. Automation + authenticity. That's the new winning formula.

By tapping into AI-powered emotional intelligence, sales teams can read between the lines, anticipate customer needs, and deliver next-level personalization that actually feels human. The result? Stronger relationships, higher trust, and a sales experience that doesn't just convert—it resonates.

But there's a fine line between enhancing human interactions and automating them too much. So, how do we strike the perfect balance?

How do we use AI to work smarter without losing the personal touch that makes sales truly impactful?

That's exactly what we'll dive into next. Let's explore how to leverage AI without losing the human edge—because the future of sales isn't just digital. It's deeply personal.

CHAPTER 10

The Pirates of Sales: Charting a New Course in the Digital World

Yo ho ho! Sales in the digital age isn't a predictable voyage, it's an epic adventure, full of shifting tides, hidden treasures, and uncharted waters. What if we reimagined modern salespeople not as buttoned-up, rule-following professionals, but as daring pirates navigating the open seas of transformation and technology?

Welcome to the **Pirates of Sales**, a fresh concept for the new era of selling. Forget the old maps. This is about rewriting the rules, embracing risk, and mastering the skills to thrive in a world where everything is digital, dynamic, and always changing.

Why Salespeople Need to Think Like Pirates

Pirates didn't survive by playing it safe. They were disruptors, innovators, and opportunists who thrived in chaos. Today's sales landscape is just as unpredictable. Buyers have endless options, AI is rewriting the rules, and traditional sales tactics are walking the plank.

To succeed, salespeople need to:

- Spot opportunities before anyone else.
- Adapt quickly to changing conditions.
- Build strong alliances to navigate challenges.
- Embrace tech as their most powerful weapon.

The Modern Pirate Code: Skills for the Digital Sales World

Like the swashbucklers of old, today's salespeople need a new set of skills to survive and thrive. Let's break it down with some pirate-inspired flair.

1. The Navigator: Mastering Digital Tools

Every great pirate had a compass, but today's sales navigators need CRMs, automation tools, and analytics dashboards. Modern sales isn't about guessing—it's about using data to chart the best course.

- **Story:** Imagine a sales rep who uses AI tools to analyze a prospect's behavior—knowing exactly when to reach out and with what pitch. The result? A deal closed before competitors even knew there was an opportunity.

Skill: Get fluent in digital platforms like HubSpot, Salesforce, and ZoomInfo. These tools are your treasure maps, showing you exactly where to find your gold.

2. The Treasure Hunter: Spotting Hidden Opportunities

Pirates didn't wait for treasure to come to them, they went out and found it. In sales, this means understanding your market, anticipating trends, and uncovering untapped potential.

- **Story:** A SaaS company noticed a rise in remote work and shifted their pitch to focus on collaboration tools. By spotting the trend early, they became leaders in a booming category.

Skill: Study market data, read the currents (trends), and always ask, "Where's the next big opportunity?"

3. The Code Maker: Building Trust and Alliances

Even pirates had their codes—agreements to keep the crew united. In sales, relationships are your lifeline. Whether it's collaborating with marketing or building trust with buyers, alliances are everything.

- **Story:** A sales rep partners with the marketing team to launch a killer campaign that targets a niche audience. The result? Higher-quality leads and faster conversions.

Skill: Develop your soft skills—empathy, active listening, and collaboration. Sales isn't just about talking; it's about connecting.

4. The Shapeshifter: Adapting to Change

Pirates thrived because they could pivot on a dime. Modern salespeople need to be just as flexible, especially in a world where AI, social media, and buyer behaviors are constantly evolving.

- **Story:** When TikTok started gaining traction, a sales rep used the platform to create fun, engaging videos that attracted leads from a younger demographic. Their company doubled its pipeline in six months.

Skill: Stay curious. Embrace new tools, platforms, and techniques as they emerge. The more adaptable you are, the more unstoppable you'll be.

5. The Storyteller: Crafting Epic Narratives

Pirates were legendary storytellers, spinning tales of adventure to rally their crews and intimidate rivals. Salespeople today need the same skill—telling compelling stories that connect emotionally with buyers.

- **Story:** A sales leader frames a pitch around a customer success story, showing how their product solved a pain point for a similar client. The prospect immediately sees themselves in the story and signs the deal.

Skill: Master the art of storytelling. Make your pitch less about features and more about the buyer's journey and how you'll guide them to their treasure.

6. The Hacker: Breaking the Mold

Pirates didn't follow rules—they rewrote them. In sales, this means questioning traditional tactics and experimenting with new ideas.

- **Story:** A startup sales team ditches cold calls for personalized video messages. The result? A 50% increase in response rates.

Skill: Be fearless. Try new approaches, learn from failures, and always keep innovating.

The Pirate's Arsenal: Tools for Modern Sales

Every great pirate needs the right gear. Here are the must-have tools for digital sales rebels:

- **AI Tools:** Use platforms like ChatGPT for personalized pitches and insights.
- **Social Media:** Build your brand and connect with prospects on LinkedIn, TikTok, or Instagram.
- **Analytics Dashboards:** Tools like Tableau help you spot trends and track performance.
- **CPQ Software:** Make complex quotes simple and error-free.

How to Build the Pirate Mindset

1. **Be Bold:** Don't wait for instructions—take the initiative.
2. **Stay Agile:** Pivot when the winds change. If a strategy isn't working, try something new.
3. **Value Your Crew:** Collaborate with your team and other departments to share insights and build stronger strategies.
4. **Keep Learning:** Technology, buyer behaviors, and markets are constantly evolving. Stay ahead by always upskilling.

Final Thought: Be the Captain of Your Own Ship

The Pirates of Sales aren't here to follow the rules—they're here to rewrite them. By embracing boldness, adaptability, and innovation, today's salespeople can navigate the digital seas with confidence and creativity.

So, grab your compass (aka your CRM), set your sails, and get ready to claim your treasure. The future of sales is yours to conquer. Yo ho ho!

Let's dive into real-world examples of salespeople and companies who've embraced the **Pirates of Sales** mindset across different regions. These modern-day "pirates" are rewriting the rules, seizing opportunities, and thriving in their markets by being bold, innovative, and adaptable.

Asia: TikTok's B2B Breakthrough in China

The Bold Move:

TikTok, known globally for short-form videos, identified a massive opportunity in B2B sales within China. While most social platforms catered to consumers, TikTok spotted a trend: businesses were using the platform to reach younger decision-makers. Instead of sticking to consumer ads, TikTok launched a B2B solution tailored to SMBs looking for creative, engaging ways to market their products.

The Pirate Move:

They didn't just offer ads—they became advisors. TikTok provided SMBs with tools and templates to create engaging content, transforming small businesses into content creators. This bold pivot opened a new revenue stream and solidified TikTok as a trusted partner in the B2B space.

Key Takeaway:

Spot trends before others and tailor solutions to meet untapped needs. In the digital world, even consumer platforms can pivot to serve businesses.

America: HubSpot's Freemium Revolution

The Bold Move:

HubSpot, a leader in sales and marketing software, turned the traditional SaaS playbook on its head by introducing a freemium model. They realized that buyers were tired of aggressive sales tactics and wanted to experience value before committing.

The Pirate Move:

HubSpot offered a free version of its CRM, knowing that once users got hooked, they'd upgrade to premium features. They also disrupted sales training by offering free, high-quality educational content through their HubSpot Academy. This approach transformed the buying journey and built unmatched trust with customers.

Key Takeaway:

Give value first. Boldly disrupt traditional sales methods by offering something useful and accessible, earning customer loyalty before asking for a commitment.

Africa: Safaricom's Mobile Money Empire (Kenya)

The Bold Move:

Safaricom, a telecom company in Kenya, identified a pain point: millions of people lacked access to traditional banking. Instead of staying in their lane as a telecom provider, they launched **M-Pesa**, a mobile money platform that allowed users to send, save, and spend money via SMS.

The Pirate Move:

Safaricom didn't just create a product—they created a financial revolution. M-Pesa brought banking to millions, and their sales strategy revolved around partnerships with local businesses to integrate the service into everyday life.

Key Takeaway:

Look for gaps in the market that intersect with your expertise. Then go all in, even if it means creating a completely new category.

Europe: IKEA's Augmented Reality Game-Changer

The Bold Move:

IKEA, the Swedish furniture giant, knew that online furniture shopping lacked one critical element: visualization. Customers couldn't picture how products would fit in their homes. To solve this, they launched the **IKEA Place** app, which uses augmented reality (AR) to let users virtually place furniture in their spaces.

The Pirate Move:

This wasn't just a tech gimmick—it was a sales strategy. By integrating AR into their buying journey, IKEA eliminated hesitation and increased online conversions. They transformed the sales pitch into an interactive, customer-driven experience.

Key Takeaway:

Use emerging technology to enhance the buying journey and solve real customer pain points. Be the first to adopt tools that set you apart from competitors.

Middle East: Noon.com's E-Commerce Ecosystem

The Bold Move:

Noon.com, a leading e-commerce platform in the Middle East, faced fierce competition from global giants like Amazon. Instead of competing on price alone, Noon focused on building an ecosystem that catered specifically to regional needs, including local language support, payment options, and delivery logistics.

The Pirate Move:

Noon launched initiatives like **Noon Mahali**, empowering local artisans and small businesses to sell online. This bold move tapped into the region's entrepreneurial spirit, creating loyalty among sellers and buyers alike.

Key Takeaway:

Lean into your local market's unique needs and build solutions that resonate with cultural and economic realities.

Final Thought: A Global Crew of Sales Pirates

From China to Kenya, Sweden to the UAE, the Pirates of Sales are thriving by thinking differently, embracing technology, and putting customers at the center of their strategies. Whether it's using AR to visualize furniture or launching a financial revolution with mobile money, these modern sales pirates show that bold moves lead to big rewards.

The question is: What's your next bold move? Are you ready to rewrite the sales playbook and navigate uncharted waters? The treasure is out there, you just have to go get it. ⚑☠

Smartketing: The Game-Changer for a Unified Sales and Marketing Future

The Old Model: Horses and Carts

Let's rewind to the not-so-distant past. Marketing was the strategist, crafting the campaigns and bringing in leads. Sales was the executor, hitting the pavement to close deals. It was a "horse and cart" relationship—marketing led; sales followed. But the wheels often fell off because the two sides weren't in sync.

Imagine this: Instead of sales and marketing pulling in different directions, they're a dynamic duo, perfectly synced, working toward a common goal. What if this isn't just collaboration but the birth of something entirely new? Enter **Smartketing**, a fresh approach that redefines the relationship between sales and marketing in the digital age.

Smartketing isn't just a buzzword, it's the new label for a world where sales and marketing merge to create a seamless, customer-focused powerhouse. It's about tearing down silos, leveraging technology, and driving results by working smarter, not harder.

Instead of sales and marketing working in silos, they now co-create the buyer's journey. Marketing generates insights and warms up prospects; sales takes over to close deals and nurture relationships. Together, they form a unified, customer-first machine.

The term **"Smartketing"** was first popularized by **John Koetsier**, a journalist, analyst, and technology thought leader. He introduced the concept to describe the seamless integration of **sales** and **marketing** to create a smarter, more efficient approach to driving business growth.

Koetsier emphasized that in a digital-first world, where customer expectations and buyer journeys are constantly evolving, traditional silos between sales and marketing needed to dissolve. The idea of Smartketing is about leveraging technology, data, and collaboration to create a unified strategy that benefits both teams—and, most importantly, the customer.

Why Smartketing?

The traditional divide between sales and marketing no longer fits the modern buyer's journey. Customers don't see two separate teams—they experience one brand. Smartketing reflects this reality by aligning sales and marketing into a single, cohesive force.

- **Unified Goals:** Forget separate KPIs. Smartketing focuses on shared metrics like customer acquisition cost (CAC), lifetime value (CLV), and overall revenue growth.
- **Shared Tools:** Smartketing means everyone works from the same tech stack, using data-driven insights to guide strategy and execution.
- **Customer-Centric Approach:** It's not about who owns the lead—it's about creating the best possible experience for the customer, from their first click to their final purchase.

The Smartketing Playbook

1. Shared Ownership of the Funnel

In the old days, marketing handled the top of the funnel (awareness and interest), while sales owned the bottom (decision and purchase). In Smartketing, the entire funnel is a shared responsibility.

- **Example:** A software company integrates its marketing automation platform with its CRM, allowing both teams to see where every prospect is in their journey. Marketing helps nurture leads all the way to the decision stage, while sales provides feedback on lead quality.

Key Move: Align your teams to focus on the full customer journey, not just their "part" of the funnel.

2. Data as the Bridge

Smartketing thrives on data. By combining insights from both teams—marketing's lead-gen metrics and sales' customer feedback—you get a 360-degree view of what works and what doesn't.

- **Example:** A retail brand uses Smartketing to analyze abandoned cart data. Marketing sends targeted emails to re-engage customers, while sales reach out with personalized offers, doubling recovery rates.

Key Move: Invest in integrated tools like HubSpot or Marketo that allow seamless data sharing and analysis across teams.

3. Technology-Driven Collaboration

Smartketing requires the right tools to succeed. This isn't just about having a CRM or marketing automation—it's about building an interconnected tech stack that empowers both teams to work together.

- **Example:** A B2B company uses AI-powered tools to predict which leads are most likely to convert. Marketing targets these leads with tailored content, while sales focuses on closing the deal with personalized outreach.

Key Move: Use platforms like Salesforce, LinkedIn Sales Navigator, and predictive analytics tools to align efforts and prioritize the best opportunities.

4. A Unified Voice

Smartketing ensures that customers hear one consistent message, whether they're seeing an ad, reading a blog, or talking to a sales rep.

- **Example:** Apple's marketing and sales teams work together to ensure every interaction reflects the brand's core values: simplicity, innovation, and quality. This consistency builds trust and loyalty.

Key Move: Develop shared brand guidelines and messaging frameworks that both teams follow.

Real-World Examples of Smartketing in Action

Spotify: Personalized to Perfection

Spotify's marketing creates hyper-personalized campaigns like "Spotify Wrapped," while sales work with advertisers to monetize this data. Together, they've created a system where personalization drives both user engagement and revenue growth.

Airbnb: Storytelling at Scale

Airbnb's marketing team crafts emotional, customer-driven campaigns that inspire travelers. The sales team then uses these stories to onboard hosts, showing how they can create similar success. This unified approach has fueled Airbnb's explosive growth.

Why Gen Z Will Love Smartketing

Gen Z buyers expect seamless experiences, personalized interactions, and authentic connections. Smartketing delivers by aligning sales and marketing to meet these expectations head-on:

- **Transparency Rules:** Smartketing ensures the entire buyer journey is smooth and consistent, with no mixed messages or hidden agendas.
- **Tech-First Approach:** Gen Z loves innovation, and Smartketing thrives on using cutting-edge tools to enhance the customer experience.
- **Purpose-Driven Messaging:** By working together, sales and marketing can tell a cohesive, value-driven story that resonates deeply with this socially conscious generation.

Building Your Smartketing Strategy

1. **Create a Smartketing Culture:** Start by fostering collaboration. Hold joint meetings, share insights, and celebrate wins as one team.
2. **Invest in Tech:** Build a unified tech stack that integrates your CRM, marketing automation, and analytics tools.
3. **Define Shared KPIs:** Align on metrics that matter to both teams, like customer retention, revenue growth, and CLV.
4. **Stay Agile:** Smartketing is about adaptation. Regularly review data, experiment with new strategies, and refine your approach.

Final Thought: Smartketing is the Future

In the digital world, where customer expectations are higher than ever, Smartketing isn't just an idea—it's a necessity. By aligning sales and marketing into a single, cohesive force, businesses can create seamless experiences, boost profitability, and build lasting customer relationships.

The question isn't whether you should embrace Smartketing—it's how quickly you can start. Because the companies that master this approach won't just survive, they'll dominate.

So, are you ready to be a Smartketing pioneer? Let's set sail.

Conclusion: Become the Captain of Your Own Sales Journey 🏴‍☠️

Sales today isn't about following a rigid map—it's about navigating uncharted waters, taking bold risks, and rewriting the rules. Just like pirates of the past, modern sales leaders spot opportunities before anyone else, embrace change, and use technology as their secret weapon. Whether it's leveraging AI, mastering digital tools, or building trust like a true crew, success comes to those who think differently and act fearlessly.

Across industries and regions, companies and individuals are proving that the Pirates of Sales mindset isn't just a cool metaphor—it's a game-changing strategy. From TikTok's B2B revolution to IKEA's AR-powered shopping experience, the real winners are the ones who take risks, disrupt norms, and adapt faster than the competition.

So, what's your next bold move? Will you stick to the old sales playbook, or will you grab your compass, raise your flag, and carve your own path? The treasure is out there, you just need the courage to go after it. Yo ho ho, the future of sales is yours to conquer!

CHAPTER 11

S.C.A.L.E. The Hack you Need to Close Faster

Let's be honest sales has changed. Buyers are smarter, faster, and have more choices than ever. If you're still relying on outdated tactics, you're basically playing a losing game. Enter S.C.A.L.E.

This isn't just another sales framework—it's a flexible, no-BS strategy built for today's fast-moving, customer-first world. It takes the best of modern sales methods and turns them into a playbook that actually works.

The goal? Make your buyers see the value, get to "yes" faster, and close deals without the back-and-forth struggle. Ready to level up? Let's break it down.

S: Simplify

- **Focus:** Buyers are overwhelmed by complexity. Simplify their decision-making process by breaking down challenges into manageable parts and presenting clear, actionable solutions.
- **How:**
  - o   Ask concise, targeted questions to uncover needs.
  - o   Provide straightforward messaging and easy-to-follow steps to move deals forward.
- **Example:** Instead of overwhelming a prospect with a product's technical details, simplify the pitch to focus on how it addresses their specific pain points.

C: Connect

- **Focus:** Build genuine relationships by understanding the prospect's unique context, priorities, and goals. Connection isn't just about rapport; it's about relevance.
- **How:**
  - o   Map the buyer's journey to align solutions with their needs.
  - o   Use conceptual discussions to understand their mental model and tailor your approach.
- **Example:** During a discovery call, actively listen and frame your solution as part of their bigger picture rather than pitching features.

A: Align

- **Focus:** Align your solution with the buyer's key business drivers, metrics, and strategic goals. Demonstrate how your offering fits seamlessly into their framework.
- **How:**
  - o Challenge assumptions and bring new insights that align with their goals.
  - o Use MEDDIC principles to identify decision-makers and their metrics of success.
- **Example:** Instead of passively reacting to a buyer's stated needs, provide insights that challenge their thinking and realign their strategy with your solution.

L: Leverage

- **Focus:** Leverage the buyer's pain points, gaps, and existing resources to create urgency and drive momentum in the deal.
- **How:**
  - o Dig deeper into the "why" behind their pain.
  - o Use the Sandler "up-front contract" to ensure mutual agreement on next steps and expectations.
- **Example:** Highlight the cost of inaction and show how their current challenges can be resolved with your solution, creating a compelling case to act now.

E: Empower

- **Focus:** Empower the buyer with the tools, confidence, and knowledge they need to advocate for your solution internally and make a decision.
- **How:**

    o   Equip champions with tailored insights and ROI models to justify the purchase.

    o   Use account-based strategies to focus on high-value prospects.

- **Example:** Provide customized ROI calculation and a slide deck they can use to pitch your solution to their stakeholders.

By using **S.C.A.L.E.**, sales professionals can streamline their approach, foster stronger relationships, and consistently achieve outstanding results. This methodology isn't just about selling—it's about helping customers succeed.

Now that we've broken down the S.C.A.L.E. sales methodology, let's see it in action. The following case studies show how these principles aren't just theoretical, they're practical, adaptable, and capable of driving real results. Whether it's rethinking a product launch or aligning with a client's strategy, these examples highlight how S.C.A.L.E. turns challenges into opportunities and moves deals forward faster.

Case study: Introducing Queso Nacho Triangles to a QSR Chain

When approaching a prominent quick-service restaurant (QSR) chain in the UAE in one of their Ideation Session, McCain Team's goal was to introduce a new product, **Queso Nacho Triangles**, as a unique appetizer. The standard process for such chains involves launching **time-limited offers (TLOs)**—new products that are tested over a three-month period to gauge their success. If the offer resonates with customers and performs well in sales, the product may be added to the permanent menu.

During an ideation session with the QSR's operations team, we discovered they were planning to launch a new flagship sandwich. This revelation led to a pivotal shift in strategy. Instead of pitching **Queso Nacho Triangles** solely as an appetizer, we proposed incorporating them as an ingredient in the new sandwich. This innovative idea aligned perfectly with the flavor profile they were aiming to achieve.

The QSR team was impressed by how the **Queso Nacho Triangles** elevated the sandwich's taste and solved their challenge of creating a memorable, balanced flavor. Ultimately, the sandwich was not only a hit during its campaign but also added to the permanent menu due to its overwhelming success.

- **Framework to the Queso Nacho Story**

S: Simplify

Focus: Simplify the client's decision-making process by presenting clear and actionable solutions.

- **How it was applied:**
    o Initially, **Queso Nacho Triangles** were pitched as a straightforward appetizer option. However, after understanding the client's plans for a new sandwich, the idea was simplified further by positioning the triangles as a flavor-enhancing ingredient for the sandwich.
    o This streamlined the decision-making process by integrating our product into an already-planned menu item, removing the complexity of marketing it as a standalone offering.
- • **Outcome:** By presenting a clear and focused solution, the client quickly recognized the added value of the product, making it easier to greenlight the idea.

C: Connect

Focus: Build genuine relationships by understanding the client's unique context and challenges.

- **How it was applied:**
  - o During the ideation session, active listening helped us uncover the client's vision for their new sandwich and the challenges they faced in creating a distinct flavor profile.
  - o By reframing **Queso Nacho Triangles** as a solution to their problem rather than an additional product, we demonstrated relevance and understanding.
- **Outcome:** This approach strengthened the relationship with the client, positioning us as collaborators invested in their success rather than just suppliers.

A: Align

Focus: Align the product offering with the client's strategic objectives and business drivers.

- **How it was applied:**
  - o The QSR chain's strategic objective was to create a blockbuster sandwich that could drive customer engagement and increase sales.
  - o By aligning **Queso Nacho Triangles** with this goal, we presented the product as an integral component of the sandwich, enhancing its appeal and ensuring its success.
- **Outcome:** The alignment ensured the sandwich not only performed well during its campaign but also became a permanent menu item, exceeding the client's expectations.

L: Leverage

Focus: Maximize opportunities by addressing pain points and capitalizing on potential.

- **How it was applied:**
  - o We leveraged the opportunity of the sandwich launch to secure a higher volume of orders for **Queso Nacho**

Triangles, as the sales of sandwiches significantly outpaced those of appetizers.

  o The QSR team was also facing a challenge in achieving the desired flavor balance for their sandwich. **Queso Nacho Triangles** offered a solution that not only met this need but also enhanced the overall product.

- **Outcome:** This approach resulted in significantly larger orders than initially expected, creating a win-win scenario for both parties.

E: Empower

Focus: Enable the client to succeed with confidence by providing tools and support.

- **How it was applied:**
  o The idea of incorporating **Queso Nacho Triangles** into the sandwich was presented with full support, including recipe suggestions, marketing ideas, and feedback mechanisms to ensure seamless integration.
  o The product's success in the sandwich campaign empowered the QSR team to confidently promote it to their customers, driving higher engagement.
- **Outcome:** The sandwich became one of the most successful menu items during its campaign, leading to its addition to the permanent menu.

Lessons Learned from the Queso Nacho Story Using S.C.A.L.E.

1. **Opportunities Are Everywhere:** Success often lies in thinking beyond traditional approaches. By exploring how **Queso Nacho Triangles** could complement an existing product, we uncovered a breakthrough opportunity.

2. **Collaboration Is Key:** Building strong relationships and listening to client challenges can lead to innovative solutions that benefit both parties.
3. **Adaptability Drives Results:** By pivoting from the original pitch and adapting the product offering, we created a solution that exceeded expectations.

By following the principles of the S.C.A.L.E. methodology, this success story highlights how understanding the client's needs, simplifying solutions, and aligning with their strategic goals can lead to exceptional outcomes in modern sales.

At the End it is important to understand that Gen Z isn't just the future — they're the present. They're redefining how brands sell, shaping entire industries, and demanding better experiences. If you can tap into their world, you're not just making a sale — you're creating a connection, building loyalty, and setting your business up for long-term success.

So, whether you're selling sneakers, streaming services, or something in between, the message is clear: **Gen Z is the revolution your sales strategy needs. Are you ready to keep up?**

How Gen Z is Redefining Sales

Traditional sales pitches? **Hard pass.** Gen Z wants real conversations, personalized experiences, and brands that speak their language. To win them over, you need to:

- **Show Up Where They Hang Out:** Whether it's TikTok, Instagram, or Discord, you've got to meet them where they are.
- **Keep It Real:** Authenticity is everything. They can smell fake a mile away, so be transparent and honest.
- **Make It Fun:** Gen Z loves brands that bring joy. Gamify your sales process, create shareable moments, and keep things interactive.

Empower Their Choices: Use data to offer personalized recommendations that feel tailor-made for them.

What Makes Gen Z Tick?

1. They're Always Online — And Expect You to Be, Too.

This is the generation that lives and breathes digital. They shop, learn, and connect online, and they expect seamless, lightning-fast experiences. If your website lags or your brand isn't on their favorite platform, you've already lost them.

2. They Demand More Than Products — They Want Purpose.

Gen Z vibes with brands that stand for something real. They're drawn to companies that care about sustainability, diversity, and making a difference. If your brand has a mission that matches their values, you're in their good books. If not, they'll swipe left faster than you can say "greenwashing."

3. They're Smart Shoppers Who Love a Good Deal.

Having grown up in uncertain times, Gen Z knows the value of a dollar. They'll hunt down the best reviews, compare options, and score the sweetest deals. It's not about being cheap; it's about being smart.

4. They're All About the Experience.

Gen Z loves brands that make them feel something. Whether it's an immersive AR shopping experience, a gamified app, or a memorable unboxing moment, they're here for the vibes.

5. **They're Creators and Innovators.**

Gen Z isn't just consuming content — they're making it. From running side hustles to designing merch, they're always creating. If you can empower their creativity, you've got a lifelong fan.

"I Am Not Here to Spend; I Am Here to Trade"

The Modern Sales Playbook for a Barter-Driven World

It was a sunny Saturday afternoon, and the city buzzed with life. Amal sat at her desk, laptop glowing with tabs of marketplaces and social platforms. But Amal wasn't just another millennial browsing for a quick buy. She had a mantra, a mindset that set her apart: *"I am not here to spend; I am here to trade."*

For Amal, the world wasn't divided into buyers and sellers. It was a community of creators, collaborators, and problem-solvers. She didn't see sales as cold transactions; she saw them as partnerships, a dance of value. And in today's digital world, that perspective is reshaping the very essence of how we sell, connect, and grow.

The Shift from Spending to Trading

Let's rewind a bit. Traditional sales was all about *spending*. The consumer paid, and the seller delivered. It was a one-way street. Efficient? Sure. Personal? Not so much.

But as technology evolved and platforms emerged, the rules changed. Sales was no longer just about the wallet—it became about the value exchange. Why? Because buyers, especially Gen Z, don't just want a product; they want experience, a connection, a story.

Platforms like Etsy, Depop, and LinkedIn aren't just marketplaces; they're stages for trading. Creators barter skills for reviews, influences trade exposure for products, and businesses swap services to save resources. The new sales mantra? "What can we exchange to create mutual value?"

The Trade Manifesto

As Amal closed her laptop that day, she smiled. The jacket she wanted wasn't just hers because of money; it was hers because she had traded her photography skills to tell a story for the seller's brand. And in that trade, a connection was born—a bond rooted not in dollars but in value.

That's the future of sales. It's not just about convincing people to spend. It's about showing them how trading value creates something bigger: trust, collaboration, and innovation.

So, the next time you pitch, remember this mantra:

"I am not here to spend; I am here to trade."

Because in the digital world, the best salespeople aren't just sellers, they're traders of value, creators of partnerships, and architects of a connected, collaborative future.

The Modern Salesperson as a Trader

Picture this: You're a sales manager pitching a SaaS platform to a startup. Instead of leading with a discount, you say, "What if we give you free access for six months, and in return, you become a case study for us?" Now the conversation shifts from "buy" to "partner." That's the power of a trading mindset.

Sales professionals today aren't just persuaders, they're matchmakers. They connect the dots, finding ways to make value flow in both directions.

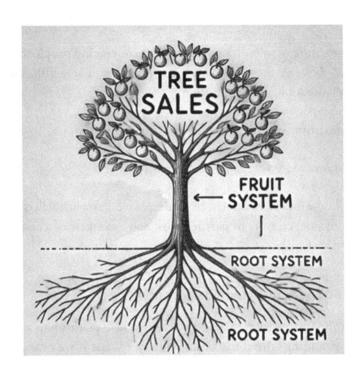

The Growth Tree Mindset: Balancing Roots & Fruits in the Digital Age

A New Era of Sales Thinking

Imagine you are walking through an orchard. The sun filters through the lush green leaves, and ripe, colorful fruits dangle within reach. But what you don't see—what lies beneath the surface—is the vast network of roots that make this abundance possible. Without a deep, healthy root system, the tree would struggle to bear fruit consistently.

Sales, much like this tree, must grow in two directions at once. A business cannot thrive by chasing quick wins alone, nor can it afford to nurture relationships endlessly without tangible revenue. The key is balance. The roots—trust, ethics, brand reputation, and long-term relationships—must be as strong as the fruit-bearing branches—revenue, market expansion, and short-term gains.

This is the foundation of the Growth Tree Sales Framework, a methodology designed for the modern, digital-first sales environment. By integrating cutting-edge tools like AI, automation, data analytics, and social selling with timeless human-centric principles like trust-building, storytelling, and emotional engagement, this framework ensures sustainable success.

The DNA of Sustainable Sales Growth

Every tree starts with a seed, and every great sales strategy starts with principles that guide every interaction. The Growth Tree Sales Framework is built on two complementary forces:

The Root System: Long-Term Strength & Trust

   a. Trust as Currency – In an era of information overload, credibility and authenticity are the true differentiators.

b. Ethical Selling – Deceptive tactics may win deals, but they erode long-term brand equity. Transparency is non-negotiable.

c. Customer-Centricity – Solve problems, don't just sell products. Customers buy outcomes, not features.

d. Brand as an Ecosystem – Your company isn't just a product; it's an experience, a philosophy, a trusted advisor.

e. Relationship Capital – Transactions are fleeting; partnerships endure.

f. Sustainable Growth – True sales success isn't measured in a quarter—it's measured in loyalty, referrals, and community impact.

The Fruit System: Short-Term Wins & Revenue Acceleration

a. Speed & Agility – The modern sales landscape changes rapidly; adaptability is key.

b. Data-Driven Decision Making – AI, analytics, and automation should inform every strategy.

c. Omnichannel Presence – Customers engage across multiple platforms—meet them where they are.

d. AI-Powered Personalization – No two buyers are alike; tailor every interaction.

e. Storytelling-Driven Selling – Facts tell, stories sell. Emotion creates connection and trust.

f. Automation for Efficiency – Free your sales force from manual work so they can focus on high-value relationships.

Key Strategies: Balancing the Root System with the Fruit System

A tree cannot survive with only roots or only fruit. Both must thrive simultaneously. Here's how to apply this principle in modern sales:

Nurturing the Root System (Long-Term Growth)

a. Trust-Driven Brand Awareness – Leverage thought leadership, educational content, and social proof.

b. Hyper-Personalized Relationship Selling – Use AI-driven insights to deepen customer connections.

c. Customer Retention Over Acquisition – Focus on repeat customers and referrals.

d. Sales & Marketing Alignment – Ensure consistent messaging across all touchpoints.

e. Sustainability as a Sales Advantage – Consumers favor brands with ethical and social responsibility.

Accelerating the Fruit System (Short-Term Gains)

a. AI-Powered Prospecting & Lead Scoring – Identify high-intent buyers faster.

b. Omnichannel Sales Engagement – Use social selling, conversational commerce, and real-time chat.

c. Agile Sales Playbooks – Train teams to respond dynamically to market shifts.

d. Emotionally Intelligent Sales Storytelling – Engage buyers through narrative-driven selling.

e. Automated Follow-Ups & Nurture Sequences – Ensure no lead is lost.

Tactical Execution: Real-World Application

Root System in Action (Long-Term Growth Examples)

- **Apple (USA):** Apple has built one of the strongest brand-root systems in the world. By focusing on design excellence, privacy-first technology, and an interconnected ecosystem, Apple creates deep customer loyalty. Its premium positioning and storytelling—through product launches and its minimalist, user-centric branding—make it more than just a company; it's a culture. The Apple Store experience reinforces this, offering highly trained specialists and immersive interactions to create an emotional connection with consumers before they even make a purchase.

- **Huawei (China)**: Huawei has invested heavily in research and development (R&D) to solidify its foundation as a global tech leader. With a deep focus on 5G technology, cloud computing, and AI, it has established itself as a powerhouse in telecommunications. The brand's strategy emphasizes long-term innovation over quick wins, positioning itself as a technological leader even amid global challenges.
- **Samsung (South Korea)**: Samsung is a prime example of a company that balances innovation (roots) and aggressive market expansion (fruits). With a multi-tier product strategy, Samsung appeals to both premium and budget-conscious customers while maintaining a consistent brand presence in flagship and mid-range markets. Samsung's long-term commitment to sustainability, foldable technology, and semiconductor advancements ensures it remains at the cutting edge, while its short-term strategies involve rapid new product launches and competitive pricing to capture quick sales wins.

Fruit System in Action (Short-Term Revenue Acceleration)

- **Tesla**: Uses AI-driven lead nurturing and referral incentives to drive rapid conversions.
- **Nike**: Engages consumers through social selling and influencer partnerships.
- **Amazon**: Leverages predictive analytics and AI chatbots to maximize efficiency.

By adapting the Growth Tree Mindset, you won't just close deals, you'll cultivate lasting success. The best sales leaders know that success isn't just about what you sell, it's about how you grow. Just like a tree, your sales strategy must be firmly rooted in trust, ethics, and long-term customer relationships while simultaneously reaching outward, generating revenue, and expanding into new markets.

This is the essence of the Growth Tree Sales Mindset: **"Roots of trust, fruits a must—nurture both, and sales will thrust"**

AFTERWORD

The Power of Sales

Sales isn't just about numbers—it's about perspective, communication, and the choices we make every day. The words we use shape our mindset, and our mindset shapes our success. Consider this:

- **Sales** has 5 letters, so does **Trust**.
- **Sell** has 4 letters, so does **Help**.
- **Lose** has 4 letters, so does **Gain**.
- **Price** has 5 letters, so does **Value**.
- **Cold** has 4 letters, so does **Warm**.
- **Doubt** has 5 letters, so does **Faith**.
- **Reject** has 6 letters, so does **Accept**.
- **Fear** has 4 letters, so does **Hope**.
- **Push** has 4 letters, so does **Pull**.
- **Risk** has 4 letters, so does **Safe**.
- **Weak** has 4 letters, so does **Bold**.
- **Noise** has 5 letters, so does **Focus**.
- **Ignore** has 6 letters, so does **Engage**.
- **Neglect** has 7 letters, so does **Connect**.
- **Rush** has 4 letters, so does **Plan**.
- **Delay** has 5 letters, so does **Speed**.

Change your words, change your world.

In sales and marketing, the words you speak, the actions you take, and the mindset you embrace define your journey. **Speak value, act with purpose, and think growth—because every choice shapes your future.**

The goal of this book is not just to share sales strategies, but to **ignite a movement**—one that embraces the evolution of sales in a digital-first world. Sales is no longer just about transactions; it's about adaptation, connection, and innovation.

To keep this momentum alive, I propose the creation of **"Future Z"** a **virtual hub of knowledge** dedicated to advancing sales theories, techniques, and best practices. This platform will serve as a **collaborative space for professionals**, where ideas are exchanged, experiences are validated, and the future of sales is shaped through continuous learning.

By fostering this **network of shared insights**, we empower individuals and businesses to **navigate market shifts**, adapt to emerging trends, and drive meaningful success.

If you're interested in being part of this initiative, reach out to us at **jvaroqa@gmail.com**.

Printed in the United States
by Baker & Taylor Publisher Services